Learning
from a
Long Walk

LESSONS FROM A FAITHFUL JOURNEY

Texas Baptist Missions Foundation

Paul W. Powell

BAPTISTWAYPRESS®

Dallas, Texas

This book was produced in cooperation with the
Texas Baptist Missions Foundation.
Bill Arnold, President.

BAPTISTWAY PRESS® Leadership Team
Executive Director, BGCT: David Hardage
Director, Church Ministry Resources: Chris Liebrum
Publisher, BaptistWay Press®: Scott Stevens

Cover and Interior Design and Production: Desktop Miracles, Inc.
Printing: Data Reproductions Corporation

First edition: August 2014
ISBN–13: 978–1–938355–26–4

To Cathy Vaught Powell.
My wife of sixty years
and the epitome of the ideal
woman described in Scripture.

"A wife of noble character who can find?
She is worth far more than rubies…
Many women do noble things,
but you surpass them all."

Proverbs 31:10, 29

A Brief History of the Texas Baptist Missions Foundation

Begun as a two-year experiment to raise additional funds for new churches, the Texas Baptist Missions Foundation has, for the past thirty years, worked with generous Baptists to support mission activities in Texas and around the world. The mission statement of the Foundation is simple:

> To the glory of God, develop innovative partnerships with followers of Christ who want to use their resources to change the world.

With that statement as the guideline, the Foundation has worked with over 33,000 different donors to support more than 250 different mission projects all over Texas and around the world. Because the Foundation is supported by the Texas Baptist Cooperative Program, every dollar of the funds given though the Foundation is used for its intended purpose. The Foundation provides $1.00 of mission money for every 13 cents of Cooperative Program money that it receives. Working with donors and forming innovative partnerships is an exciting challenge. Those partnerships have included providing funds to build operating rooms for a Baptist hospital in Mexico, developing a no-interest loan program for low-income churches, helping start more than a twelve hundred new churches, building and equipping a tool trailer for the Texas Baptist Men retiree builders, building a community center in Japan, and building four Baptist Student Ministry buildings on college campuses—just to name a few.

The ways that donors funded these projects are as varied as the projects themselves. Many were funded by gifts of cash or stocks and bonds. For others, a charitable trust that provided income to the donor and spouse was the best method of achieving their goals. Sometimes there were gifts of a tangible asset—like land—that provided the needed resources.

"To the glory of God" is an important part of the Foundation's mission statement. That is the reason the Foundation exists and the goal of every visit with a donor and the goal of every partnership that receives funds. It is a great joy for the staff to work with people who want to make a difference in Texas and around the world, and to do it to God's glory.

The Texas Baptist Missions Foundation is a part of the Baptist General Convention of Texas.

▬ May We Help You? ▬

If you would like to explore ways you can make a difference for God's kingdom with a portion of your resources, the Missions Foundation can help. No matter the size of your gift, the Foundation staff is willing to help you use it in whatever way you feel the Lord leading. Whether by making a gift of cash or other asset, establishing a trust, or giving something through your will, we can assist you in selecting the best method for you to accomplish your giving goal. If you would like to explore the possibilities, give us a call at (800)558-8263 or visit our website at www.texasbaptists.org/tbmf.

Table of Contents

Introduction

*A*ccording to Scripture, "The length of our days is seventy years—or eighty, if we have the strength; yet their span is but trouble and sorrow, for they quickly pass, and we fly away" (Psalm 90:10). At this writing I am beyond my promised allotted days. All in all it's been a fun run. Much of it has been uphill and I have had my share of valleys. But, whatever the road conditions, I have always been "pressing on the upward way."

When I left the pastorate after thirty-four years to become President/CEO of The Annuity Board of the Southern Baptist Convention (now Guidestone Financial Resources), I intended to serve until retirement. Then I planned to go back to East Texas and ride off into the sunset. Obviously the Lord had other plans.

After three years of retirement, with an abundance of preaching engagements, I was asked to become the dean of George W. Truett Seminary at Baylor University in Waco, Texas. In order to accept that position I had to resign as a regent of the university. When I did, a fellow regent gave me a CD of Randy Travis' songs. One of them was, "Don't Ever Sell Your Saddle 'Cause Life is a Long, Long Ride."

That's what I had done. I thought I was at the end of the trail and I had sold my saddle. The Lord was telling me to mount up and ride farther. This time it was a six-and-a-half-year ride. Maybe the most important of my ministry.

I have often said, "I'm like an old tennis ball. I've been batted around a lot. I've lost much of my bounce. But I'm still in the game." That's worth something.

I've learned a few things along the way—things about God, myself, and the church. Obviously I think these are things worth sharing. That's what this book is about. If you want to know the details you will have to read on. If you ask anyone who knows me, they will tell you that I (like a well-known television commentator) am a simple man. What I have to say is not hard to understand or to apply to life.

This is not my first book, but it is my last. Russell Dilday jokingly tells people that I once asked him, "Have you read my last book?" And he replied, "I hope so." Well, stop hoping, this is it.

I can't see as well as I once did, but I can see well enough through my bifocals to know that the finish line is not far ahead. I've had some great examples and mentors along the way so my prayer is,

> "Therefore, since we are surrounded by such a great cloud of witnesses, let us throw off everything that hinders and the sin that so easily entangles, and let us run with perseverance the race marked out for us. Let us fix our eyes on Jesus, the author and perfecter of our faith . . ."
>
> HEBREWS 12:1–2A.

I do want to finish well.

Paul Powell
Tyler, Texas
April 9, 2014

1

Walking with God

Since my youth, O God, you have taught me, and to this day I declare your marvelous deeds. Even when I am old and gray, do not forsake me, O God, till I declare your power to the next generation, your might to all who are to come. Your righteousness reaches to the skies, O God, you who have done great things. Who, O God, is like you?

Psalm 71:17–19

A man asked a lady, "How old are you?" She replied, "My age is my business, why do you ask?"

He responded, "Looks like you've been in business a long time."

You can look at me and tell that I have been in business a long time. Some people try to roll back the odometer and cover up their age. Not me! I want you to know why I look the way I do. I've traveled a long way in life and some of the roads were unpaved.

Besides, about the time you reach sixty-five everything begins to wear out, fall out, or spread out. I often say, "I feel like an old tennis ball. I've been batted around a lot. I've lost most of my bounce, but I'm still in the game!"

There are lots of problems associated with old age. You can't see as well as you once did, hear as well as you used to, and your recall is slower. A priest was walking down the street one day and saw a little boy with a lawn mower that had a sign on it which read, "For Sale." He stopped and asked the boy how much he wanted for the lawn mower. The little boy replied, "Thirty dollars."

The priest said, "Well, we need a lawn mower down at the church and that looks like a pretty good one." The young man said, "It is." The priest then said, "What are you going to do with the money?" The little boy replied, "I'm going to buy me a bicycle."

So the priest bought the lawn mower. A day or two later the little boy was riding his new bicycle by the church and the priest was trying to start the lawn mower. He pulled and pulled and pulled but just couldn't crank it. When he saw the little boy, he called him over and said, "Son, I thought you said this was a good lawn mower. I can't get the thing started."

The little boy said, "Father, it is, but I forgot to tell you that you have to cuss it to get it to start." The Father replied, "Well, son, I haven't cussed in years and I have forgotten all the words I knew."

The little boy replied, "Well, you pull on that thing long enough and they'll come back to you."

That's the way my memory is. If you'll just give me enough time I can think of things. But they do come slower than they used to.

And those aren't the only problems. You spend a lot more time in the doctor's office. Now days, when I go to the doctor they ask me two questions they used to never ask. They want to know, "Do you dread going home?" And, "Have you fallen lately?"

The first time the nurse asked me, "Do you dread going home?" I responded, "Why do you ask that?" She replied, "It's required by law. There are some people who are abused at home." I then said, "Has somebody been telling you about my wife?" Then I quickly said, "No, there's no place I would rather go on this earth than home."

Then they ask, "Have you fallen lately?" My answer up until now had always been the same, "No." But that's not exactly true. I did fall some time ago but I don't tell about it.

My wife had not been feeling well and called out from the bathroom that she thought she was going to faint. I rushed in and stooped down in front of her. I told her to lock her arms around my neck and I would put my arms under hers and lift her up and walk her to the bed.

I intended to walk backwards holding her up so she could lie down until she felt better. But just as I got her on her feet, she fainted and fell to the floor. With her arms locked around my neck and my arms under her arms, she pulled me down on top of her.

She was unconscious for only a few seconds. When she regained full consciousness she said, "Am I in heaven?" I answered, "I hope not because I'm on top of you." She then revived and I got her up and into the bed and she was OK. You don't think I told the nurse about that do you? There are some things that should be kept between a man and his wife.

But in spite of all the problems related to aging, we ought not resent getting old . . . some people are denied the privilege.

One advantage of getting old is that we have had a chance to walk with God for a long time and to learn from him, and about him. That was the experience of the psalmist in Psalm 71:17–19. This is the prayer of an old man who has walked with God since his youth. He has faithfully told others of God's wondrous works and great power. But now that he's old and gray, he fears he will outlive his usefulness. No one wants to do that.

So he asks the Lord to not put him on the shelf or turn him out to pasture, but to keep using him in his service.

He wants to tell the next generation the things he has learned from his long walk with God. He wants to remain useful to the Lord.

The fear the psalmist felt is shared by many senior adults. They fear that they are no longer useful or have a contribution to make to God or to society.

There is no reason why any person, young or old, should ever feel that there is nothing left for them to do; nothing to contribute to life. We can always tell others of God's grace and glory no matter our age. People may think we are out of touch or behind the times because we don't understand all the modern technology of this generation. But the fact is, human nature has not changed since Adam and Eve; and *God never changes*. So there will always be a place, a lifelong place, for us to share the wonderful works of God.

I have walked with God for sixty-five years and he has had a long time to teach me about himself. But, then, I had a lot to learn. I didn't know Job from job, Revelation from revelations.

I did not grow up in a Christian home. Though we lived in the shadow of two churches, we never went to church. We never read the Bible, never prayed, never spoke of spiritual things. So I knew virtually nothing about God. Mark Twain once described a man as ". . . ignorant as the unborn babe! . . . ignorant as unborn twins!"[1] That's the way I was.

But through my long walk with God; I have learned some things about his wondrous works, his power, and his strength that are worth passing on to you. They are simple truths, but they can change your life if you grasp them fully.

) God moves in mischievous ways his wonders to perform.
) You can be too big for God to use, but you can't be too small.
) God doesn't save us from the trials of life, he sustains us in them.
) God will save from the guttermost to the uttermost those who come to him.

━ The Invisible Hand of God ━

First, God moves in mischievous ways, his wonders to perform.

I know that's not how the poet William Cowper first wrote it. He said, "God moves in mysterious ways, his wonders to perform."

Cowper was subject to fits of depression. One day he ordered a cab (they were horse drawn carriages in those days), and he told the driver to take him to the London Bridge. Soon a dense fog settled down upon the city. The cabby wandered about for two hours and then admitted he was lost. Cowper asked him if he thought he could find the way back home. The cabby thought that he could, and in another hour landed him at his door.

When Cowper asked what the fare would be, the driver felt that he should not take anything since he had not gotten his fare to his destination. Cowper insisted on paying the cabby saying: "Never mind that, you have saved my life. I was on my way to throw myself off the London Bridge." He then went into the house and wrote:

> God moves in mysterious ways,
> His wonders to perform.
> He plants His footsteps on the waves,
> And rides upon the storm.[2]

I have a friend whose maid, trying to recall those famous lines, said, "God moves in *mischievous* ways; his wonders to perform." Say it however you will, mysterious or mischievous, God does move in our lives.

There is in life what Adam Smith called "the invisible hand of God."[3] It is the unseen hand of Providence leading, guiding, and directing things in our lives to bring his will to pass. And because it is invisible, we see it only with the eye of faith or as we look back on life.

I have experienced some of God's mischievous ways in my life. In 1972 I was pastor of the First Baptist Church in San Marcos, Texas. One Sunday, members of the pastor search committee of the Green Acres Baptist Church in Tyler, Texas visited our services.

The next week the chairman called to ask me to meet with the entire committee to discuss becoming their pastor. After a couple of meetings they asked me to preach in view of a call. I agreed, and after preaching in their morning service, they voted in the evening service to extend a call to me to become their pastor.

We were back in San Marcos by that time so the chairman, Leo Chesley, called after the vote to give me the news, and to ask if I would accept their call. I was not sure I was ready to leave San Marcos, so I asked them to give me a week to pray about it.

By the end of that week I was still undecided, so when Mr. Chesley called again I asked for yet another week. I loved San Marcos and didn't want to leave my friends, but I tried to be open to the Lord's leading. I prayed more earnestly than I had ever prayed about anything in my life. I was so in agony that I actually prostrated myself on the floor of my study. I'm not sure why I did that except I had read in the Bible of people prostrating themselves before the Lord in great distress.

Lying there I said, "Lord, I don't know what to do." Then I said, "Lord, I'm going to Tyler if you don't put up a roadblock that a blind man can see. Lord, I don't want to be presumptuous, but I'm going to Tyler if you don't stop me."

The next day I received a telephone call from Bob Kertchiville, president of the largest savings and loan in town, who wanted to visit with me. He asked, "Paul, what would it take to get you to stay in San Marcos?" I responded, "Bob, all I want to do is God's will." He responded, "Suppose we build you a new home?" I responded, "No, Bob, I just want to do what's right." I walked away from his office wondering, "Lord, is that the roadblock I asked for?" But I quickly dismissed the idea because I was convinced that that was not the way God works.

We moved to Tyler, rented an apartment, and began building our first home. My friends in San Marcos knew the difficulty I had in making the decision. Almost every week I received a telephone call or a letter from someone saying that I should come back to San Marcos where I belonged.

My best friend, Ronnie Wilson, was chairman of the pulpit committee and he was one of those who called often asking me to consider coming back. Every call made my life more miserable. I was really homesick for San Marcos.

Early in November, just a few weeks before our new home was to be completed, I told Cathy, "I'm going back to San Marcos." My good wife usually knew God's will before I did. She never tried to influence me, but this time she urged me to not consider going back; but I was determined.

It was Wednesday afternoon and I made multiple calls to my friend Ronnie before and after prayer meeting to tell him I was ready to come back. I was never able to reach him. When I finally reached him on Thursday morning to tell him I was ready to come back to San Marcos, he said, "Oh Paul, we met last night and invited a pastor to come in view of a call."

I hung up the phone and said to myself, "Lord, there's the roadblock I asked for, not to keep me from going but to keep me from going back." From that day on I settled down and had peace about being in Tyler. If I had gone back to San Marcos, it would have been the biggest mistake of my life. I was following my heart—not his will; and he stopped me.

The Scriptures say, "The king's heart is in the hand of the LORD; he directs it like a watercourse wherever he pleases" (Proverbs 21:1). So is the heart of the preacher. My heart was back in San Marcos and it needed to be turned to Tyler . . . and the Lord did it in one fell swoop.

Listen to the Scriptures, "Trust in the LORD with all your heart and lean not on your own understanding; in all your ways acknowledge him, and he will make your paths straight" (Proverbs 3:5–6).

I have learned through the years that when we cannot trace the hand of God, we can trust the heart of God. His hand may be invisible, but we can trust that he is present in our lives.

▬ Looking for Availability and Reliability ▬

Second, we can be too big for God to use, but we can't be too small.

When the Lord was looking for a king to replace the failed Saul, the only qualification he mentioned was seeking a man "after his own heart" (1 Samuel 13:14, Acts 13:22). He didn't go to the palace to find a prince, or to the tabernacle to choose a priest, or to the military compound for a general. He rather "took" a fourteen-year-old shepherd boy from the sheepfold and made him the king of Israel (2 Samuel 7:8). Why did he do that? I think it was to show that: *you can be too big for God to use, but you can't be too small.*

God is never impressed with our strength or self-sufficiency. He is drawn to people who are weak and admit it. The great missionary J. Hudson Taylor said, "All God's giants have been weak men, who did great things for God because they reckoned on His being with them."[4]

Moses is a case in point (Exodus 3–4). He was born the child of an Israelite slave in Egypt, adopted by Pharaoh's daughter, and raised in the royal palace. One day he saw an Egyptian abusing an Israelite slave and in anger slew the man. When his crime was discovered he fled the country as a fugitive from justice.

When God came to him, he was tending the sheep of his father-in-law on the back side of the desert in the land of Midian. The circumstances of life had humbled him and when the Lord told him he had been chosen to lead the Israelites out of bondage, he came up with more excuses than a Baptist deacon being asked to lead a stewardship campaign.

His first excuse was, "Who am I that I should go to Pharaoh? Lord, I'm a nobody" (Exod. 3:11). His second excuse was, "I don't know what to say. I don't even know your name" (Exod. 3:13). His third excuse was, "If I go and tell them the Lord has sent me, they won't believe me" (Exod. 4:1). His final excuse was, "Lord, I am slow of speech, I'm not eloquent. I stutter. I have a hard time getting my thoughts and words out" (Exod. 4:10).

When he had exhausted all of his excuses the Lord said, "Good, Moses! You're just the kind of man I'm looking for. I will be with you and you will do just fine." He did that, I believe, to show us: *you can be too big for God to use, but you can't be too small.*

When the Lord called Gideon to deliver Israel from the Midianites, Gideon responded by saying, "Lord, I am the youngest member of the poorest family of one of the most insignificant tribes in Israel. You must have made a mistake" (Judges 6:15). And the Lord must have said, "Gideon, I've done more with less. You're my man." The Lord picked Gideon, I believe, to show us: *you can be too big for God to use, but you can't be too small.*

When the Lord called Jeremiah to be a prophet to the nations, Jeremiah tried to excuse himself saying, "Lord, I can't speak, I'm just a child" (Jeremiah 1:6). The Lord responded, "Jeremiah, I don't call the qualified, I qualify the called. You'll do just fine." The Lord picked Jeremiah, I believe, to show us: *you can be too big for God to use, but you can't be too small.*

The Apostle Paul, in describing the makeup of the early church, said, "Brothers, think of what you were when you were called. Not many of you were wise by human standards; not many were influential; not many were of noble birth" (1 Corinthians 1:26). It is not ability but availability and dependability that God is looking for.

The Lord took Moses from the back side of the mountain and he took me from the back alleys of Port Arthur and made me into a minister. He did these things to show that he can use anyone of us in his service if we will let him. He can turn our weakness into strength. The fact is: *we can be too big for God to use, but we can't be too small.*

Peter advises Christian workers, "Humble yourselves, therefore, under God's mighty hand, that he may lift you up in due time" (1 Peter 5:6). There's the hand of God again—the same hand that holds the heart of the king exalts the humble.

It is not ability; but availability, dependability, and humility that the Lord is looking for and uses.

▬ Life's No Fairy Tale ▬

Third, the Lord doesn't save us from the trials of life, he sustains us in them.

Troubles are a part of life. They come to all of us. The Scriptures say, "Yet man is born to trouble as surely as sparks fly upward" (Job 5:7). And again, "Man born of woman is of few days and full of trouble" (Job 14:1).

Grace Kelly, the American-born actress and Princess of Monaco, said, "The idea that my life is a fairy tale is itself a fairy tale." That's true of all of us. Carlyle Marney said, "The trouble is life just won't lie down and behave."

Nowhere does God promise that if we follow him we will live longer, be healthier, be more prosperous, or have better kids. He does promise to be with us and see us through. His promise is, "When you pass through the waters, I will be with you; and when you pass through the rivers, they will not sweep over you. When you walk through the fire, you will not be burned; the flames will not set you ablaze" (Isaiah 43:2).

The Lord does not promise to keep us out of difficulties but rather to see us through them. He does not promise to *isolate* us, but to *insulate* us.

If you aren't careful you'll miss verse one of the chapter. It says, "But now, this is what the LORD says—he who created you, O Jacob, he who formed you, O Israel: 'Fear not, for I have redeemed you; I have summoned you by name; you are mine'" (Is 43:1). Think of that, the Lord knows your name. Then he promises to be with us in our difficulties.

When trials come it's OK to cry, Jesus did. It's OK to lean on your friends, Jesus did. It's OK to ask God to take it away, Jesus did. It's OK to question God, Jesus did . . . just so long as you come to the place where you say, ". . . yet not my will, but yours be done" (Luke 22:42). And "Father, into your hands (there are those hands again) I commit my spirit" (Luke 23:46).

One of the paradoxes of Christianity is that the One who could not carry his own cross is the One who enables us to carry ours.

▬ From the Guttermost to the Uttermost ▬

Fourth, the Lord can save from the guttermost to the uttermost those who come to him.

The Scriptures, in describing for us the priestly work of the risen Christ say, "Wherefore he is able to save them to the uttermost that come unto God by him, seeing he ever liveth to make intercession for them" (Hebrews 7:25, KJV).

The word "able" in the original language is the word from which we get our word *dynamite*. It's speaks of the power and strength of God to save us. The word "save" literally means to rescue from both the power and the penalty of sin, and the domination and damnation it brings.

Sin gets a grip on us. It easily becomes our master and we its slave. But Christ has the power to break the grip of Satan and set us free. He frees us not only from the power of sin, but from its penalty which is eternal damnation. He is able to save us to the "uttermost" i.e., *to the very end.* There's an old saying, "He can save from the guttermost to the uttermost." He can reach down to the depths to lift us up. And he can keep us safe until the end of time; if we will turn to him by faith and trust.

Josh Hamilton of the Anaheim Angels baseball team is a case in point. At the 2012 All-Star break, he was arguably the most popular player in baseball. He got fifty percent more votes than anyone else in the sport. Out of high school he was the number one pick in the 1999 major league draft.

But Josh was given to cocaine addiction and never reached his potential. He was in and out of rehabilitation not one time, not two times, but eight times. By then he was considered hopeless.

Josh was banned from baseball, and a judge's court order prevented him from returning to his home with his wife and children. So he showed up at the doorsteps of his grandmother's house at two o'clock in the morning. He had nowhere else to go. He said, "My grandmother had said I could always come to her anytime for any reason. So I wound up on her doorsteps."[5] It was on those doorsteps, reading the Bible; that Josh shortly thereafter gave his life to Christ and eventually climbed back into baseball.

Commenting on his popularity as an all-star he said, "I feel like people understand who I am and what I stand for, that I love Jesus. This gives me a platform to better talk about him."

God not only reached down to the depths to pluck out Josh Hamilton, but he will do the same for you and me. He not only can save us from the depths but he can keep us safe until the end.

Listen to Jesus, "My sheep hear my voice, and I know them, and they follow me: And I give unto them eternal life; and they shall never perish, neither shall any man pluck them out of my hand. My Father, which gave them me, is greater than all; and no man is able to pluck them out of my Father's hand" (John 10:27–29, KJV).

There is the hand of God again—keeping us safe as well as guiding us.

And there is no safer place to be than in God's hand.

The key thought in those verses is, ". . . Jesus is able to save to the uttermost those who come to God by him."

When we come to Jesus we discover that the same hand that guides us in life; the same hand that lifts us in his service; the same hand that comforts us in our sorrow; is the same hand that holds us safe for all eternity.

And there is no safer place to be than in the hands of God.

The poet put it like this:

> The hands of Christ seemed very frail
>   For they were broken by a nail,
> Only they reach heaven at last
>   Whom those frail, broken hands hold fast.
>
> —JOHN RICHARD MORELAND—"HIS HANDS"

We must come by faith and put our hand of faith in the nail-scarred hand of Jesus and we will be saved.

—————————————— N O T E S ——————————————

1. Mark Twain, *Roughing It* (1886), 321.

2. L.B.E. Cowan, *Springs in the Valley* (Grand Rapids: Zondervan, 1939), 274–275.

3. Adam Smith, *The Theory of Moral Sentiments* (1759), 184–185.

4. J Hudson Taylor, *Hudson Taylor's Choice Sayings: A Compilation from His Writings and Addresses* (London: China Inland Mission, n.d.), 29.

5. Susie Magill, "It's a God Thing," *Sharing the Victory*, October 2008, http://bit.ly/1pajr4p.

2

Seeing God

Yet he has not left himself without testimony: He has shown kindness by giving you rain from heaven and crops in their seasons; he provides you with plenty of food and fills your hearts with joy.

Acts 14:17

A little boy and his grandfather were sitting on a dock in the late afternoon fishing. They talked about many things—why sunsets are red, why rain falls, why seasons change, why clouds are white, and what life is like. Finally, the boy looked at the old man as he was baiting his hook for him and asked, "Does anybody ever see God?" "Son," said the old man looking across the blue water, "It's getting so I can hardly see anything else."

In my long walk with God I've learned to see him more often and more clearly than ever before.

Someone once said, "No man is so blind as one who will not see." God is clearly seen by those who look through the eyes of faith. The passing of the years does not dim our ability to see things eternal.

I can see how a person could be an agnostic and say, "I do not know if there is a God." But I cannot understand how a person can be an atheist and say with absoluteness, "There is no God." Agnosticism is a claim of *ignorance*. Atheism is a claim of *arrogance*.

If a person should say to me, "There is no God," I would ask, "Have you been everywhere there is to go? Have you seen everything there is to see? Do you know all there is to know? Have you had every experience there is to have?"

No one has been everywhere, seen everything, had every experience, or possesses total knowledge. So, unless he is intolerably arrogant, he would have to answer, "No!" to those questions.

I would then suggest to him, "Perhaps, then, God is to be found in one of those places you have never been. Maybe he is to be known in that particle of knowledge you do not yet possess. Maybe God can be seen and felt in one of those experiences you have not yet had." For a person to claim, "There is no God" is to claim more than any person can possibly know. A little humility might help.

Faith in God is so evident it is universal. When Columbus first came to the new world, the Indians had religious rites and observances for the afterlife and a belief in the immortality of the soul.[1] We have never found a civilization where people did not have a religion or a belief in God (or a god.) We have found civilizations without coliseums, without theaters, and without schools. But we have never found a civilization without religions.

Atheism is more often emotional than intellectual. Those who study atheist and agnostic college students have found that they have "reported more anger toward God during their lifetime than believers."[2] They often had some type of disappointing experience in life: they didn't get into the school they wanted to; they had a sports injury; a family member died; they suffered from hunger as a child; or were the victim of a terrible natural disaster. These people have a hard time understanding how a "good God" could possibly allow such things, and so, the average atheist is born.

Strange isn't it, to get mad at someone we don't believe exists?

Interestingly, the Bible never tries to prove the existence of God. It begins with the tremendous avow, "In the beginning God created the heavens and the earth" (Genesis1:1) and thereafter the non-existence of God is never considered. There is only one verse in the entire Bible (repeated twice) that addresses the subject of atheism. It reads, "The fool says in his heart, 'There is no God'" (Psalm 14:1, 53:1). The Hebrew word for "fool" literally means "stupid." I don't mean to be insulting, but I agree with John Wayne, "Life is tough. It's even tougher if you're stupid."

Atheism leads not so much to *badness* as it does to a life of *sadness*. When an atheist sins, he has no place to go for forgiveness; when gratitude wells up within him, there is no one to thank; in the day of trouble, there is no one to lean on; when standing before an open casket or a freshly dug grave, there is nothing to hope for. The poet expressed it best when he wrote:

> O, to have no Christ, no Savior
> How lonely life must be.
> Like a sailor lost and driven
> On a wide and shoreless sea.
> O, to have no Christ, no Savior
> No hand to clasp thine own
> Through the dark, dark veiled shadows
> Thy must press thy way alone.[3]

Today, even with bifocals, I see God more clearly than ever before.

Here's why: creation, conscience, and experience.

> ⟩ Looking around . . . at creation.
> ⟩ Looking within . . . at conscience.
> ⟩ Looking up . . . in faith.

▬ Seed Time and Harvest ▬

The most obvious evidence for God, the one in clear view of everyone, is nature itself.

This is the evidence the Apostle Paul pointed to in his first sermon to a pagan audience (Acts 14:17). When he spoke to Jews (who already believed in one God) he started with the Scriptures; but when he spoke to pagans, he began with nature.

Paul and Barnabas were on their first missionary journey. In Lystra they encountered a man who had been crippled all of his life. Perceiving the faith of the man, Paul commanded him to stand up and the man was miraculously healed. The people of Lystra thought Paul and Barnabas were gods who had come down among them and wanted to offer sacrifices to the missionaries. Paul quickly stopped them and encouraged them to turn from their worthless, helpless gods to the living God who made all things.

He then reminded them that though God had allowed the nations to follow erroneous religious superstitions, "he had not left himself without a witness in the world, in that he did good, gave us rain from heaven and fruitful seasons, filling our hearts with food and gladness" (Acts 4:17, KJV).

The word "witness" is used in the judicial sense. It means "to give testimony, to present evidence." Paul then pointed to seed time and harvest as evidence of God. He did not point to the towering redwoods of California; nor to the majestic mountains of Colorado; nor to the vast starry skies of Texas. He rather pointed to the tiny seed as evidence for, and testimony to, God.

A seed is both a miracle and a mystery. There are over 300,000 different kinds of plants and trees. Each one has some type of seed and every seed has the germ of a new plant in it. When planted in the soil, watered by the rain, and warmed by the sun; given sufficient time, the seed will germinate and grow.

As someone has said, "All the flowers of all the tomorrows are in the seeds of today." Seeds under the right conditions can survive and still "come to life" and grow after thousands of years.

Paul's argument here is simple. We have a world on our hands, a wonderful, fruitful world, where seeds produce plants and plants produce food and all our needs are met. All of this begs an explanation. Where did it come from? How did it get here?

We have two choices, either it made itself or someone else made it. There are some people who believe the world made itself. They tell us that eons ago life spontaneously emerged from lifeless matter and then evolved into the world as we know it today. Life sprang from death and then evolved from the simple to the complex so that everything you see now came about on its own.

George Orwell once said that some ideas are so foolish that only an intellectual could believe them. This is one of them. The idea of a thing making itself is absurd when applied to anything else. For example, there's a beautiful pulpit where I preach. If you asked me where it came from and I said, "It made itself," you would say to me, "That's nonsense. A pulpit couldn't make itself. It had to have someone make it." If a pulpit cannot make itself, how could anything as complex and orderly as a seed, much less the universe make itself? It is this simple, "God made heaven and earth and everything therein."

Nature not only declares the reality of God, but it also shows us his nature. The Scriptures say, "For since the creation of the world God's invisible qualities—his eternal power and divine nature—have been clearly seen, being understood from what has been made . . ." (Romans 1:20). Much of what can be known of the invisible God can be seen and understood by what he made.

Think of that pulpit again. It is over 100-years-old, built in 1883 for the First Baptist Church of Tyler, Texas. Though we have never seen the man who made it, we can know a lot about him from what he made. For one thing, we know he was alive. A dead man couldn't build it. We know that he had intelligence, because a baboon couldn't build it. We know that he was a skilled craftsman. An amateur couldn't make it. And we know that he was an artist because it is a beautiful piece of work. We don't know everything about him from what he made, but we do know a lot.

What does the seed teach us about God? It teaches us that he is powerful. Only God can make a seed. Man with all his genius cannot put life in a seed. We know he is wise. Seeds need soil and sunshine and water to grow. God thought of everything. We know he is gracious. He "gave" seeds to us as an act of his grace. That's why humble people say "grace" to thank him before we eat.

The fact is that we have a wonderful world made by a powerful, gracious, and wise God. What he created is a witness to his glory and power.

Seed time and harvest do not tell us anything about salvation, our redemption from sin. It will remain for Christ to do that. But it does tell us a lot. If first century men had reason to believe in God because of creation, we have even more. We have both the telescope and the microscope to view the world that he made. Lee Rogers, as quoted by Bob Murphy in the *Minneapolis Star,* said, "If the molecules in one drop of water could be converted into grains of sand, there would be enough sand to build a concrete highway, half a mile wide and one foot thick, from New York to San Francisco."

When the people of the first century looked up into the heavens, they could count 5,000–6,000 stars. But today, by the means of the telescope, we know that there are at least 100 billion stars in our galaxy and at least 10 billion galaxies as big as ours in space. Walter F. Burke, who managed the Mercury and Gemini Space Projects said, "The further we penetrate into space, the more I am confronted with the wisdom and majesty and omnipotence of God."

He goes on to say, "I know some people are saying that God is dead. But it is not the scientists who are saying it. Though I have known hundreds of scientists involved in space work, I have never met one who considered himself an atheist. Our faith is strengthened, rather than jeopardized, by the exploration of space."

Everywhere we look in creation we see order, design, and purpose. To believe that this just happened by accident would require more faith than I have.

It has been told that once while sailing the Mediterranean, the men in Napoleon's suite were discussing God. During the talk, the men eliminated God altogether. Napoleon had been silent, but at the end of the conversation he pointed at the sea and sky and said, "Gentlemen, who made all this?"

The idea that life sprang from nothing is not science but philosophy. Science deals with what can be observed, proven, and tested by experiment. Creation happened only once, and can't be repeated. No one was there to see it but God. We must take his word for it or guess at it. At best, evolution is a guess; a hypothesis; an assumption. That's why we call evolution a *theory.*

Comedian Dennis Miller, when asked if he believed in God, replied, "I believe somebody made Darwin (the scientist). Yes, and I bend my knees to God and pray." So do I. Creation itself behooves all of us to take the posture of humility and bow before the God of all life.

There had to be an intelligent mind behind Creation. Common sense demands it. It couldn't have just happened. So, the Scriptures say, "The heavens declare the glory of God; the skies proclaim the work of his hands" (Psalm 19:1).

A Still Small Voice

Second, if you want evidence of the existence of God, look within your conscience.

Emanuel Kant, the German philosopher (1724–1804) wrote in *The Critique of Practical Reason*, "Two things fill the mind with ever new and increasing admiration and awe, the more often and steadily we reflect upon them: the starry heavens above me and the moral law within me."[4]

There is, in every person, a sense of right and wrong. It is innate, inherent, and instinctive. We did not invent it and we cannot seem to escape it. Where does this sense of "oughtness" come from? It is impossible that an impersonal force could implant a moral consciousness within us. It had to come from God and it is an evidence of him.

It is that moral imperative within us, an imperative that we did not invent and cannot escape, that convinces me there is a God. There is no other way to understand it or explain it. It came from him.

The Apostle Paul stressed the universality of man's accountability to God. He first indicts the Jews, who have the law of God written in stone and on scrolls of papyrus. Then he declares that the Gentiles are just as accountable because they have God's law written on their hearts. We call it the instinctive knowledge of right and wrong (i.e., conscience).

Man is the only creature that has a conscience. A dog doesn't. Leave meat on the kitchen cabinet and the dog will eat it without a tinge of conscience, because he has none. A mad bull will gore his owner as quickly as anyone else and be unbothered by it. It is because he has no conscience. But man is different. He knows right from wrong.

Some people say there is no such thing as right and wrong. But, if that is true, why do we feel guilty when we do wrong? Why do we make excuses for our failures? Or why do we quarrel?

The late C.S. Lewis reminds us that we have all heard people quarrel and say things like, "How would you like it if someone did that to you?" Or, "Come on now, you promised." Or, "It's not fair."

The interesting thing about these remarks is that the person who makes them is not merely saying that the other person's behavior does not please him. He is appealing to some kind of standard of behavior which he expects the other person to know about and adhere to. There is no use trying to prove another wrong unless there is some sort of agreement as to what is right. There would be no sense in saying that a football player has committed a foul unless there is some agreement about the rules of the game.

Other people say that what we believe about right and wrong is learned behavior, i.e., we have been taught about it by others: our parents, the church, or society in general. That may be true of some of the content found in our conscience, but it certainly does not explain the existence of our conscience.

Again, C.S. Lewis, professor of Medieval and Renaissance English at Cambridge (who was once an agnostic) reminds us of some of the common threads that run among all people. For example, think of a country where people were admired for running away in battle, or where men feel proud for double-crossing the people who had been kindest to them. You might as well imagine a country where men are admired for putting themselves first. Selfishness has never been admired anywhere.

Men may differ as to whether you should have one wife or four, but they have always agreed that one must not simply have any woman he likes. Lewis goes on to say, "Would it surprise you to know that through the scriptures of the world's leading religions runs a single theme, expressed in an astonishingly similar form. It is the Golden Rule. This is no cause to doubt the Christian faith. It is an evidence that God has been at work among all people and written his love in their hearts."

What's behind these laws that keep pressing us, urging us, seeking to guide us? If they give instruction it must be for some mind, not matter. Impersonal matter can't give instructions. It can't teach morality. They must come from a person . . . and that person is God.

━ He Found Me ━

Finally, if you want to know God, look outside of yourself in humility and faith.

When we've said all of the above, we still have not proven God. We've only established a high degree of probability for his existence. You can't put God in a test tube or reduce him to a mathematical equation anymore than you can quantify a mother's love, a soldier's patriotism, or an athlete's enthusiasm.

There is a step beyond where you cannot go intellectually. We come to know God personally only by *faith in Christ*. The biggest obstacle to knowing God does not lie in answering all of our intellectual questions. It lies in our *will*. If we do not know God, it is because we cannot reach a decision. We will not make up our minds to follow Jesus Christ. He is the way, the truth, and the life and no one comes to God except through him. To know him is to know God because, as he said, "I and the Father are one." (John 10:30).

Some things can be known only by experience. One of them is married love. You can never know it until you have experienced it. You have to get married before you can know it.

It is the same with knowing God. You must experience him to know that he is. So to know that God is, we must take a step of faith. Blaise Pascal, the French scientist and mathematician, said, "Faith is God felt by the heart not by the reason. The only adequate knowledge is revelation. Natural theology has its place only to the believer who has already seen God at work in nature."[5]

Knowing God then is a matter of the heart, not reason. William Wilberforce, the great British reformer who was instrumental in bringing about the eradication of slavery in the British Empire, came to a point in his life when through the witness of John Newton he rediscovered the faith of his childhood. He mentioned this to one of his servants, and the servant said, "O, you have found God?" He responded, "No, I think God found me."

That's what happened to me. I was a fourteen-year-old kid wandering the streets of a seacoast town when God found me. I wasn't looking for him but he came looking for me. And, when he found me, he changed my life forever.

Was that just my imagination or was it a divine encounter? I think it was a divine encounter. It happened sixty-five years ago and I have never been able to get away from it. As someone has said, "Anything so profoundly felt must inevitably be." For me it was profoundly felt and still resonates in my soul.

What happened to me has happened to many others. The daughter of Joseph Stalin, the cruel and despicable dictator of the Soviet Union, was not a likely candidate for conversion. Her father and other Communist leaders labored for years debunking religion and trying to eradicate it from life.

But she came to Christ in her adult life. She said, "I was brought up in a family where there was never any talk about God. But when I became a grown up person I found that it was impossible to exist without God in one's heart. I came to that conclusion myself, without anybody's help or preaching. But that was a great change because since that moment, the main dogmas of Communism lost their significance for me."

God found her as he found me, and he will find you if you will open your heart to his son Jesus Christ.

In the final analysis, you must make up your mind about Christ.

He is the only way to God.

NOTES

1. Laurence Bergreen, *Columbus: The Four Voyages* (New York, New York: Penguin Books, 2011), 186, 209.

2. http://thechart.blogs.cnn.com/2011/01/01/anger-at-god-common-even-among-atheists/. Accessed 5/21/2014.

3. From "No Hope In Jesus," *Words:* William O. Cushing, in *Welcome Tidings: A New Collection of Sacred Songs for the Sunday School*, by Robert Lowry, W. Howard Doane & Ira D. Sankey (New York: Biglow & Main, 1877), number 37.

4. http://plato.stanford.edu/entries/kant-development/#ChiStaSky-AboMeMorLawWitMe. Accessed 5/28/2014.

5. Blaise Pascal, *Pensees*, 392.

3

The Word of God

For the word of God is living and active. Sharper than any double-edged sword, it penetrates even to dividing soul and spirit, joints and marrow; it judges the thoughts and attitudes of the heart.

Hebrews 4:12

A young preacher once said in a sermon, "The Bible says it, I believe it, and that settles it." An older, more seasoned preacher corrected him. He said, "That's not exactly right. The truth is, God says it, that settles it, and it doesn't matter whether you believe it or not."

The longer I live, the more convincing proof I see that the Bible is God's word; and that it can be trusted in all of its parts. It was given to us by inspiration and teaches us what we are to believe and how we are to live.

Is the Bible really the word of God? Can we trust the Bible? Whether or not the Bible is the inspired word of God is not an academic question. The whole Christian faith depends upon the answer. Only if we know that the Bible is God's word can we be sure of its teachings regarding the love of God, the forgiveness of sins, the resurrection of the body, and life everlasting.

If the Bible is not the word of God, then we must, to use the words of Plato, "Take the best and most irrefutable of human theories, and let this be a raft upon which we sail through life—not without risk, unless we can find some word of God which will surely and safely carry us."

If the Bible is not the word of God, then its teachings join the other babble of opinions which men have uttered.

On what basis can I know for certain that the Bible is not a book of myths, but is the trustworthy word of God? It is often argued that we can know the Bible is the word of God because it says so. The writers of the Bible claim repeatedly that God gave them their material. Two thousand times in the Old Testament they made this claim. Oftentimes it was to their peril. They made this assertion about 500 times in the New Testament. So, either God did speak to them as they wrote by inspiration, or they perpetuated one of the greatest frauds of all time.

To argue that the Bible is the word of God because it claims to be; is to argue in circles. Unless I first accept by faith that this book is the word of God; I have no reason to believe what it says about itself, anymore than I should believe what it says about God or anything else. Besides, there are other books which also claim to be the word of God, mainly the Koran and the Book of Mormon.

Is there some way then, apart from the fact that the Bible says so itself, to believe that this is the word of God? The answer is a resounding yes! You can trust the Bible for three reasons:

>) It has the ring of truth.
>) It has the impact of truth.
>) It has the satisfaction of truth.

━ It Authenticates Itself ━

First, the Bible can be trusted because it has the ring of truth.

If a man finds a stone and wonders if it is a real diamond, the thing to do is to take it to a jeweler and let him examine it. If it is a genuine, authentic diamond, it will authenticate itself. Examination of the stone in question will reveal its real worth.

If a man is shopping in a used furniture store and finds a piece of furniture that he thinks is a genuine antique, he must examine it to tell for sure. He must let an antique dealer look at the furniture in question. If it is genuine it will bear the marks of authenticity.

By the same token, the place to begin in determining if the Bible is God's word is with the book itself. If it is really what it claims to be, it will authenticate itself. It will have the marks of genuineness within it. It will be different from all other books.

The New Testament, given a fair hearing, does not need me or anyone else to defend it. It has the ring of truth for anyone who has not lost his or her ear for the truth. And, as the famous preacher Charles Spurgeon said, "The Bible does not need defending it just needs preaching. It is like a lion. You don't need to defend a lion. Just turn it loose and it will defend itself."

The problem is that skeptics do not bother to look at the book itself. The most important event in human history is politely and quietly bypassed. It is not as though the evidence has been examined and found unconvincing; it has simply never been examined.

What is there about this book that is different? For one thing, it has both amazing diversity and unity. It was written by over forty different people, from every walk of life, from many different countries, over a period of 1,500 years. Yet out of this diversity there is an amazing unity.

The Bible begins with the creation of the universe and moves to the end of time. It all fits together like the pieces of a jigsaw puzzle, making a complete picture. How can you explain this apart from a divine architect? This is not true of other books. It's not true of the Koran. It is a series of incoherent visions supposedly given to Muhammad in a cave by Allah. The Koran is a one-man show. The visions came to Muhammad alone. No one else was there. No one else heard or saw what he claims. All we have is his word for it.

The same is true of the Book of Mormon. Supposedly the angel Moroni appeared to Joseph Smith and guided him to golden plates where the Book of Mormon was written in hieroglyphics. Though he could not read hieroglyphics, he translated them into English, strangely enough King James English. No one ever saw the plates or the angel Moroni except Joseph Smith. Once again it was a one-man show.

Not so with the Bible. It is the result of many to whom and through whom God spoke over fifteen centuries.

Then there is the matter of prophecy. No other religion on earth has a prophet except the biblical religion. There are many prophecies in the Old Testament, clearly understood by the people of the First Century; that found their fulfillment in Jesus Christ. To declare a thing shall come to pass long before it happens, and to bring it to pass: this is nothing but the work of God. To know the future is God's prerogative alone. No man can foresee the future; not a minute from now, not a day from now, much less a thousand years from now.

Winston Churchill, former Prime Minister of England, once quipped, "I always avoid prophesying before hand, it is a much better policy to prophesy after the event has already taken place." He was a wise man and he understood that the future is the prerogative of God alone. Prophecy is one of the clearest marks of the authenticity of the Bible. It's one reason why we can trust the Bible.

Then too, if you were making up a fictitious story that you wanted people to believe, this is not how you would do it. Take the Gospel accounts of the life of Christ. There are so many things left out that an ordinary biographer would have included.

For example, we have no idea of the physical stature of Jesus; whether he had a powerful or a soft voice; we have no information about his childhood, adolescence, or young manhood. There is simply no record of the influences that helped form his character. These are the things you would ordinarily put in the story of a man's life, especially if you were building a fictitious one you wanted people to believe.

And strangely enough, having missed so much of the life of Jesus, each of the four Gospel writers spend one-third of their space telling us almost every detail of the last seven days of Jesus' life. It is as if they were emphasizing the fact, "This man came to die," which indeed he did.

In short, if the Gospel writers were inventing such a character as Jesus, they would not have set down such artless and vulnerable accounts. It is perfectly clear that they were not in conspiracy together, or they would have been careful to avoid minor contradictions and discrepancies. The truth is: *this story is too fantastic not to be true.* If you were making up a story, this is not the way you'd do it.

And if the story could have been discredited, it would have been back then. It could have easily been checked out at that time. The early disciples of Jesus went out making some amazing claims. They claimed that God had become man and that he died on a cross as a common criminal to redeem us from our sins. Then they claimed that on the third day he was raised from the dead. Their message had amazing results.

Those messengers were threatened, imprisoned, beaten, and even put to death; but, they steadfastly maintained that what they preached was true. They died for it. Ordinarily liars do not become martyrs. They recant before the execution is carried out.

We moderns tend to underestimate the intelligence of people like the Apostle Paul. Because he never saw a television, talked on a cell phone, or traveled by jet; we look down on him (and other biblical characters) as having lived in the twilight zone. While they never had access to our gadgets and technology, they did know that the dead do not ordinarily come back to life again.

We forget that they lived at a point in time close to the historical events described in the New Testament. They had plenty of opportunity to check the authenticity of the story from many eyewitnesses. As Paul said to King Festus, "The king is familiar with these things, and I can speak freely to him. I am convinced that none of this has escaped his notice, because it was not done in a corner" (Acts 26:26).

The crucifixion of Jesus was a public event. The news of his resurrection was widespread. This all occurred out in the open, not in isolation. The facts were well-known and could have been easily corroborated.

I do not know why those of us who live 2,000 years later should call into question events to which there were so many eyewitnesses. There were hundreds of them who were still living at the time when most of the New Testament was written (1 Corinthians 15:1–8). It is accurate history on a par with any other event of that era. It is a record of events that could easily have been verified in the first century.

The Bible is no fairy tale.

Yes, you can trust the Bible.

▬ The First Book I Would Burn ▬

Second, the Bible has the impact of truth.

No other book has had as great an impact on the history of man as the Bible. It is the all-time best seller, most translated, and most circulated book in history. The King James Version of the Bible has so shaped English language, art, literature, and music that no man can claim to be truly educated without a good knowledge of it.

The Bible has impacted individuals in that it turns sinner into saints. Examples are to be found everywhere. Here is a just such an example.

Years ago Dr. Robert Gehring, who at the time was a practicing gynecologist at Baylor Hospital in Dallas, Texas, spoke in the church I pastored. In his testimony he said he had become a drug addict and an alcoholic. During his addiction he came to such a point of despair that he determined to take his life. He went to the delivery room to give himself an overdose of sodium pentothal. But even as a physician, he didn't know that you can't give yourself enough of the drug to kill yourself before you pass out.

He collapsed on the floor of the delivery room where he was found by a fellow physician. The friend who rescued him was a Christian. He introduced Robert to Christ, and got him into a Bible study. In his testimony Dr. Gehring said, "In my alcoholism and drug addiction I spent $30,000 on psychiatrists, and found my help in a ten dollar Bible."

Listen. When you find a Bible that's falling apart, it usually belongs to a person who isn't.

It was Christ who made the difference in this man's life, but it was the Bible that brought him to Christ. Jesus said, "You diligently study the Scriptures because you think that by them you possess eternal life. These are the Scriptures that testify about me, yet you refuse to come to me to have life" (John 5:39–40).

In the Scriptures Jesus invites us to come to him for both eternal life and abundant life. Listen again to his last invitation, in almost the last verse of the last book of the Bible, "The Spirit and the bride say, 'Come!' And let him who hears say, 'Come!' Whoever is thirsty, let him come; and whoever wishes, let him take the free gift of the water of life" (Revelation 22:17).

The Bible has also transformed nations. It has freed slaves, lifted womanhood, cared for children, built hospitals, and fostered education. Wherever it has been believed and practiced, the world has been made better.

These accomplishments are indeed notable. Even if the Bible was destroyed, these achievements could be erased. History cannot be rewritten. Surely this has not all flourished as a result of a lie. I cannot believe that all this righteousness has triumphed by belief in a fraud. That would be a greater miracle than the Bible records. Find me another book, if you can, with such a record of achievement.

The simple fact is, and I will say it again in the next chapter, if the Bible and Christianity are not true, a lie has done more good than the truth has.

It has had to withstand the assault of tyrants the world over. It has been said that a man is known by his friends. But, he is also known by his enemies. One of the reasons we know that the Bible is such a good book is that so many bad people have opposed it. Tyrants and dictators cannot tolerate the Bible.

These enemies desire to outlaw the Bible altogether, and they have repeatedly tried to accomplish this. They know you cannot long enslave Bible-reading people. "The Bible has been," according to Thomas Huxley, "the Magna Carta of the poor and oppressed."[1] It creates in people a discontent with anything less than freedom. That's why it has been so hated throughout history.

In 2002, Liz Ngan, Old Testament professor at Truett Seminary, visited her native China. She told me upon returning, "In China, Bibles cannot be sold in bookstores, only in churches. The law prohibits two kinds of literature from being sold in public—pornographic and seditious. The Bible is not pornographic, so it must come under the category of seditious. They are afraid that it will lead to a revolution, to sedition."

Quentine Reynolds said it best, "If I were a dictator, the first book I'd burn would be the Bible."[2] That is exactly what they have done.

The tooth of time has gnawed away at the Bible, but it has stood the test of time. With all of its skeptics, the Bible has never bowed its head to a discovery of science nor to a recovery by an archeologist. The more advances these sciences make, the more they affirm the reliability of the Bible.

Yes, you can trust the Bible!

— It Speaks to My Stomach —

Finally, the Bible has the satisfaction of truth.

Why should rulers as powerful as those of China or Russia or Cuba fear a book as old and as seemingly harmless as the Bible? The fact is, it is alive, powerful, and transforming (Hebrews 4:12). People hear the voice of God through it.

The Bible speaks to the deepest needs of our lives. We need forgiveness and the Bible tells us that "If we confess our sins, he is faithful and just and will forgive us our sins and purify us from all unrighteousness" (1 John 1:9). We need meaning and purpose in our lives and Jesus tells us, ". . . I have come that they may have life, and have it to the full" (John 10:10); and we need hope and Jesus tells us, "And if I go and prepare a place for you, I will come back and take you to be with me that you also may be where I am" (John 14:3).

The Old Stone Age Indian in the jungles of Central America put it best. When he heard the Scriptures in his own language for the first time he exclaimed, "Ah, that book, it speaks to my stomach."

J.B. Phillips, whose book *The Ring of Truth* provided some of the ideas for this chapter, tells that as he began his translation of the New Testament epistles, he was continually struck with their vitality and power. "Again and again as I carry that translation" he said, "I felt like an electrician who was rewiring an ancient house without being able to turn the main power off."[3]

The purpose and the secret of the Bible's power is that it brings us to Jesus Christ. If I read it and follow it, I am soon brought to the Savior. Whatever leads me to him must be divine.

John says, "He came to that which was his own, but his own did not receive him. Yet to all who received him, to those who believed in his name, he gave the right to become children of God" (John 1:11–12).

The moment we accept Christ is the moment we become children of God. If I am God's son, why should I not recognize his voice, no matter how faint it might be? My earthly father has been dead for many years. But if I should hear his voice today, I would immediately recognize it. It is the same with the voice of my Heavenly Father.

Jesus said, "My sheep listen to my voice; I know them, and they follow me" (John 10:27).

Obviously his sheep recognize his voice when they hear it.

From my own experience I know this is the word of God.

I have heard the voice of my father, the Good Shepherd, speaking to me through its pages.

And I have followed him.

--------------------- N O T E S ---------------------

1. Thomas S. Huxley, *Essays Upon Some Controverted Questions* (New York: D. Appleton and Company, 1893), 39.

2. http://thisibelieve.org/essay/16923/. Accessed 5/21/2014.

3. J.B. Phillips, *Letters to Young Churches: A Translation of the New Testament Epistles* (London: Macmillan, 1947), 12.

4

Obeying God

. . . while evil men and impostors will go from bad to worse, deceiving and being deceived. But as for you, continue in what you have learned and have become convinced of, because you know those from whom you learned it, and how from infancy you have known the holy Scriptures, which are able to make you wise for salvation through faith in Christ Jesus. All Scripture is God-breathed and is useful for teaching, rebuking, correcting and training in righteousness . . .

2 Timothy 3:13–16

The longer I live the more clearly I see how the Bible cuts across the grain of our modern society. Years ago a pastor friend and I were discussing our upcoming sermons. He asked, "What are you preaching about Sunday?" I replied, "I'm preaching about divorce."

He responded, "Divorce! I could never do that. Half the people in my congregation are divorced." I responded, "If I preached only on the sins my people didn't commit then we could ask people to stand at the beginning of the service and sing 'God Be With You Till We Meet Again' and dismiss and go home."

Though it hurts at times, it is our responsibility to tell the truth; regardless of what the people might do.

For 3,500 years, the Ten Commandments have been the basis of our traditional moral values. But today, everywhere you look you can see the moral, spiritual, and ethical fabric of society unraveling. A large part of the reason for this is that we have abandoned our moral and spiritual foundations.

Our political and religious leaders don't help. They are supposed to be the guardians of public morality, but politicians act as though there are no standards; and if standards exist they don't apply to them. They have become lapdogs instead of watchdogs. Our preachers act like they have spiritual lockjaw. After all, nobody wants to be called a "prude", or a "fanatic", or "politically incorrect."

We've come to the place in our society where the only thing immoral *is to call anything immoral.* We've come to the place where about the only thing considered wrong is to judge anything wrong. By the way, to say that a person is wrong to call anything wrong is in itself a moral judgment. The one who makes that statement is setting himself up as the ultimate authority of right and wrong.

The truth is, everyone believes in right and wrong. A man may steal from his company and think that's OK; but if he goes out in the parking lot and someone has stolen his car, well that's a different matter altogether. A man may be unfaithful to his wife and think that's acceptable. But if she does the same thing, as we say in East Texas, "That old dog won't hunt." Follow people around and eventually you will hear them describe a situation by stating, "That's not fair." When a person uses that statement they are appealing to some standard that they believe everyone ought to know and accept.

So the question is not, do we believe in right and wrong; but what is right or wrong? And who decides? There are five possible sources to consider:

First, let every individual decide for himself/herself. That's the surest way to chaos. What would happen if we allowed each individual to decide on their own about traffic laws? There would be wrecks everywhere. To let the individual decide moral issues is the surest way to produce "moral wrecks." The "Dark Ages" of Israel's history was during the period of the judges. Twice in the Book of Judges (and once in Deuteronomy 12:8) we are told that the era was characterized by the fact that, "everyone did as he saw fit" (Judges 17:6, 21:25).

Maybe we could decide by public opinion. Just take a poll. We take polls on everything else. If we did that, however, we'd have to take a new poll every week because people are always changing. Suzanne Collins, author of *The Hunger Games* trilogy has observed; "But collective thinking is usually short-lived. We're fickle, stupid beings with poor memories and a great gift for self-destruction."[1]

Indeed the public is fickle, relying on the opinions of others instead of using eternal truths to shape beliefs. Society is treading on very thin ice that has already begun to crack. Following public opinion can (and usually does), lead to moral, social, and political anarchy.

Can we look to the law to guide us? There's no more consistency in the law than there is in individuals, or society as a whole. What is legal often depends on the bias of a judge or the pressure applied to politicians by lobbyists and special interest groups.

What about the church? The church is as confused as the rest of society. Recently in England, an Anglican priest told his parishioners that poor people struggling to survive should steal food and other essentials from shops rather than raise money through prostitution, burglary, or mugging. He said, "My advice, as a Christian priest, is to shoplift."[2]

But, at least he set down strict guidelines. He said, "I would ask that (people) do not steal from small, family businesses but from large national businesses, knowing that the costs are ultimately passed on to the rest of us in the form of higher prices. And I have asked them not to take more than they need and for any longer than they need."[3]

Most major denominations in American are being torn asunder over the question of gay rights—ordaining gay ministers and performing same sex marriages. You can't trust the church any more than you can trust the individual, society, or the law. So where then are we to go for guidance in matters of right and wrong?

We come eventually to the Bible as the only safe authority for life. John Wesley, who was often at odds with the Anglican Church, said concerning Protestants, "They traded an infallible church for an infallible Bible." He refused to accept the infallibility of the church, but he believed that the Bible as God's word was true and trustworthy. It was for him, and is still for us, a sure guide for right and wrong.

It is as simple as this: right is right because God said so; and wrong is wrong because God said so. If a thing was wrong yesterday, it's wrong today; and if the world lasts another thousand years, it'll still be wrong. And if a thing was right yesterday, it is right today; and when the stars in the heavens are but cinders in eternity, it will still be right.

The church may be confused about right and wrong, but the Bible and God are not. The Bible is not confused about the nature of marriage. It is one man and one woman committed for life.

The Scriptures are not confused about gay lifestyle. It was the sin of homosexuality that led to the destruction of Sodom and Gomorrah. That's where we get the name of the sin of sodomy. Repeatedly in both the Old and New Testaments God tells us this is wrong (Romans 1:26–28, 1 Corinthians 6:9, 1 Timothy 1:10).

The Bible is not confused about sex. It is sex under the seal and shield of marriage or total abstinence. It's not confused about pornography. "But I tell you that anyone who looks at a woman lustfully has already committed adultery with her in his heart" (Matthew 5:28).

It's not confused about drugs. The common drug of that day was wine but the Scriptures say, "Wine is a mocker and beer a brawler; whoever is led astray by them is not wise" (Proverbs 20:1).

The Bible is not confused about lying. Jesus said, "Simply let your 'Yes' be 'Yes,' and your 'No,' 'No'; anything beyond this comes from the evil one" (Matt. 5:37). In other words, say what you mean and mean what you say.

That's the truth of our text. The Apostle Paul is encouraging Timothy in his Christian living. He reminds him that he's known the Scriptures since he was a child and that they are "able to make you wise unto salvation." That's the first purpose of Scripture: to point us to Jesus, who can save us when we put our faith in him.

Then Paul says, "All scripture is given by inspiration of God and has value for the things we are to believe, pointing out error in our lives, redirecting us in life, and teaching us how to be righteous. And the ultimate goal is that the man of God would become mature, fully grown, and be all that God created us to be."

The Bible then, is our ultimate authority. It is the only safe authority for our lives. Three things need to be said about this authority:

> It is a divine authority.
> It is a spiritual authority.
> It is a liberating authority.

▬ The Breath of God ▬

First, the Bible is a divine authority.

Paul writes, "All scripture is given by inspiration of God . . ." (KJV). What does that mean? The word "inspired" means "God-breathed." During the winter we can breathe on a pane of glass and our breath congeals into crystals of ice. Likewise, God breathed on men and it crystallized into the Scriptures.

Peter helps us to understand inspiration more clearly when he tells about holy men who spoke as they were "moved" (KJV) by the Holy Ghost (2 Peter 1:21). The Greek word for "moved" means "to be picked up and brought along." The same word is used in Acts to describe what happened to the ship the Apostle Paul was traveling on to Rome.

The ship was caught in a violent storm, and it had appeared as though it would be dashed against the rocks. In an effort to save the ship and their own lives, the sailors threw the cargo overboard to lighten the load. They wrapped ropes around the hull to strengthen it, lowered the sails, and prayed as the ship was "driven" by the wind (Acts 27:17). The word "driven" and the word "moved" are translations of the same Greek word.

Like the wind that pushed that ship and drove it forward; so the Spirit of God came upon men and moved them, drove them, and pushed them to write the Holy Scriptures. The men who wrote the Bible were men upon whom the Spirit of God came with such force that they were compelled to write what they wrote.

What is the scope of inspiration? It encompasses the totality of Scripture. "*All* scripture" is given by inspiration. The sentence construction in the original language is such that the word "all" signifies "every single part of the whole." Inspiration is as broad as Scripture itself. Each part of it is from God.

Some people want to believe that parts of the Bible are inspired and other parts are not; so they can choose which parts they believe are true. But if you believe part of the Bible and reject part of the Bible; it's not the Bible you believe, but yourself.

How do we know that the Bible is inspired? Do we have any evidence other than the fact that it makes the claim about itself? We know that it's inspired because it speaks to the soul of man. It searches us and makes us realize we need help, and it offers us help.

How does a person know they are in love? They just know it. When you read the Bible you just know that it is God speaking to you. If you have not lost your ability to ascertain truth, you will recognize it when you read his word.

━ Not a Rule Book ━

Second, the Bible is a spiritual authority.

Why did God give us the Scriptures in the first place?

The Bible is not a book of science, history, math, or biology; although it contains some of all of these. It is a book of religion with a two-fold message: It is given to teach us how to be saved, and to tell saved people how they should live as followers of Jesus Christ.

The psalmist wrote, "I have hidden your word in my heart that I might not sin against you" (Psalm 119:11). Jesus hid God's word in his heart and it guided him in his hours of temptation.

Immediately after his baptism, Jesus was led into the wilderness to be tempted by the devil. Three times Satan came to him. Satan tempted Jesus to turn stones into bread, to cast himself from the pinnacle of the temple, and to fall down and worship him. Each time Jesus refused the temptation by saying, "It written . . ." Written where? Not in *Reader's Digest*. It was written in Scripture. Because Jesus knew the Scriptures, he knew right from wrong and could resist temptation. The Bible is not a rulebook like a golf, football, or baseball rulebook. Those books cover every conceivable situation in which a player might find himself. In golf, if the ball lands next to a tree, there is a rule as to what you are to do. If it lands on the cart path, the rules tell you how handle that situation. If the ball goes into the water, the rulebook tells you where to place the ball for your next shot. The rulebook covers every conceivable situation. The Bible is not such a rulebook. It does contain some specific rules, but it is primarily a book of great principles. It guides us so that we can know the answers to every issue in life.

Robert E. Lee was one of the greatest leaders in American history. He commanded the Confederate forces in the Civil War, but he was first offered command of the Union Army and turned it down. He could not bring himself to fight against his native Virginia.

After the war he was still held in the highest esteem by both North and South. As a result, Lee had many offers for work. The representative of an insurance company came to Lee to proffer the lead presidency of its concern at a salary of $50,000 a year. Lee thanked the man but said he must decline, as he was not familiar with such work.

"But, General," the man said, "you will not be expected to do any work. What we wish is to use your name."

"Do you not think," Lee replied, "if my name is worth $50,000 a year, I ought to be very careful about taking care of it?" And Lee turned the job down.

Then he was offered the presidency of Washington College, a small school in Virginia that had only about forty students. The salary was $125 a month. Lee took it and led it well. In time, the school's name was changed to Washington and Lee University.

Lee was tolerant of the young student's college pranks. He told one new student who asked for a copy of the rules, "Young gentleman, we have no printed rules. We have but one rule here, and that is that a student must be a gentleman."[4]

They all understood how a gentleman was to act. They didn't need rules; they needed a principle to guide them.

The Bible is a book full of principles that provide guidance for life, even for areas that are not specifically addressed. When asked to identify the great commandment, Jesus responded that it was to, "'Love the Lord your God with all your heart and with all your soul and with all your mind'. This is the first and greatest commandment. And the second is like it: 'Love your neighbor as yourself.'" (Matt. 22:37–39). If you will let those two great principles guide you, you will never go very far astray.

Love God consistently.

Love others consistently.

**Those great principles
will guide us in all of life.**

— No Attempt to Restrict —

Third, the Bible is a liberating authority. The purpose of Scripture is not to restrict us, but to help us reach our full potential. It is given so that the followers of Christ might be "perfect" (i.e., mature) and become all God created and saved us to be.

If a policeman stops you for speeding, or for not stopping at a stop sign, or for not fastening your seatbelt; he is not trying to restrict you. He's trying to keep you from killing yourself or killing someone else; or from causing a pileup that will leave all kinds of collateral damage. It is for your benefit that he expects you to obey the law.

It is the same with Scripture. It is for our benefit, our good, and our well-being. Consider this: If forty percent of babies are born out of wedlock, does that strengthen society? Does it give those children a better chance in life than if they were born into a family with a loving father and mother?

If millions of babies are aborted every year, does this increase the sanctity of human life? And if a twelve-year-old girl is allowed to get an abortion without the permission of her parents, does that strengthen parental authority?

If we move step-by-definite-step to approve same sex marriage, does that strengthen traditional marriage or render it meaningless? If it is no longer marriage between a man and a woman, what's wrong with polygamy? Incest?

If a student is allowed to use foul language in front of, and sometimes directly with a teacher or other adults, is it conducive to an atmosphere of discipline and respect that is necessary for effective education? If marijuana is legalized, will it lead to less use and more safety in society? A medical doctor speaking against it said, "Availability is the mother of use." Make it more available and you'll increase its use and all the evils that accompany it.

The bottom line is that God's word is designed to teach us what to believe and how to live *because it is how life works best*. If we will honor it and follow it, we will find this to be true in our own experience.

I believe like Martin Luther, who once wrote:

> Feelings come & feelings go
> and feelings are deceiving.
> My warrant is the Word of God
> Naught else is worth believing.
>
> I'll trust in God's unchanging Word
> Till heaven & earth shall sever.
> For though all things shall pass away
> His Word shall stand forever.

In the preface of one of his sermons, Wesley wrote:

> I want to know one thing—the way to heaven; how to land safely on that happy shore. God himself has condescended to teach the way; for this very end he came from heaven. He has written it down in a book. O, give me that book

at any price, give me that book of God. I have it. Here is knowledge enough for me. Let me be a man of one book.[5]

As I've grown older, I too have become a man of one book when it comes to questions of right and wrong. By God's grace we have it. So let's read it, and heed it, and we will live and die a better person. And the world will be a better place.

─────────── N O T E S ───────────

1. Suzanne Collins, *Mockingjay* (New York, NY: Scholastic Inc., 2010), 379.

2. http://www.dailymail.co.uk/news/article-1237470/Priest-advises-congregation-shoplift.html. Accessed 5/21/2014.

3. Ibid.

4. Gene Smith, *Lee & Grant: A Dual Biography* (New York, New York: McGraw-Hill Book Company, 1984), 300.

5. Arnold Lunn and Lincoln MacVeagh, *John Wesley* (New York, New York: The Dial Press, 1929), 291–292.

5

The Reach of God

After Jesus had finished instructing his twelve disciples, he went on from there to teach and preach in the towns of Galilee. When John heard in prison what Christ was doing, he sent his disciples to ask him, "Are you the one who was to come, or should we expect someone else?" Jesus replied, "Go back and report to John what you hear and see: The blind receive sight, the lame walk, those who have leprosy are cured, the deaf hear, the dead are raised, and the good news is preached to the poor. Blessed is the man who does not fall away on account of me.

Matthew 11:1–6

I suppose everyone who has lived as long as I have has eventually run into someone who believes one religion is as good as another. My first such encounter came several years ago. The man had been in the Navy and had been stationed in many countries with different cultures and different religions.

He had noticed that these religions all had some things in common with Christianity. They all had a human founder whose name they bore; a place of worship—a temple, synagogue, mosque, or church; sacred scriptures; and holy men—priests, rabbis, preachers, imams. Since they all had these common elements, he concluded they were all equal and that one was as good as another.

We must admit that other religions do have much in common with Christianity. In fact, all seven of the world religions have some form of the Golden Rule in them, "Do to others as you would have them do to you" (Luke 6:31). This should not surprise us, after all God has always been at work among *all* people. He has written his law in the hearts of *all* men. This is what we call "general revelation." We'd be surprised if this were not true.

While we have much in common with other religions, there is a deep cleavage between other religions and Christianity. Religion is man reaching up to God. Christianity is God reaching down to man. Religion is man-made. Christianity is heaven-sent. Salvation in all other religions is earned by being good or by being religious. In Christianity, salvation is by grace. It is through the goodness of God. *So Christianity is the reach of God . . . his reaching out to us.*

Humans are incurably religious. We have never found a civilization yet that did not have some form of religion in it. We have found civilizations without coliseums, without theaters, and without schools; but never have we found one without religion in it. That's because man has been made in the image of God and is created to have a relationship with God. So, instinctively man reaches up to God.

We are much like a child who has never known their earthly father. DeMarcus Ware, the outstanding Denver Bronco football player, tells that his parents split when he was only three-years-old. As a result, he did not have a relationship with his father until he was eighteen. He said this concerning his experience, "My mom and I are very close, but something was missing in my life until I was able to start having a relationship with my dad. When you don't have a dad in your life, you feel disconnected."[1]

Without God, something is always missing in our lives. We too, feel disconnected. But in our case, our Heavenly Father didn't leave us, *we left him.* But while we left him out of our lives, we couldn't get him out of our hearts. There was always a longing to have a relationship with him. That's why Blaisé Pascal (who discovered the vacuum) said, "There is a God-shaped vacuum in our hearts." And why Augustine, the great theologian, said, "Our hearts are restless until they find rest in thee."[2]

While God let us go, he left clues of himself; footprints in the sands of time so that we always knew he was there. As Paul tells us in Scripture, "In the past, he let all nations go their own way. Yet he has not left himself without testimony" (Acts 14:16–17a).

Religion is our effort to reconnect with God. Christianity is God attempting to reconnect with us. Imagine two great walls, precipices, or cliffs with a bottomless and impassable chasm separating them. On one side is God; on the other side is man. Beginning with Adam, the erosion caused by sin over the centuries cut deep and wide this great abyss separating us from God.

We longed for God and set about to build a bridge—or bridges across to God. These "bridges" we call religions. And they go by many names. But they all have two things in common: (1) they are built by people, and (2) they all fall short. Not one of them reaches the other side.

On the other side is God. With a broken heart he surveys our condition and our futile efforts. He determines that he will build a bridge to us. He carefully laid the foundation and when the fullness of time had come, he sent forth his Son.

Using the cross of Calvary as his bridge, God spanned the chasm of sin and made the way open for us to come to him. Jesus boldly declared, "I am the way and the truth and the life. No one comes to the Father except through me" (John 14:6). He became the bridge between heaven and earth, between God and man. Jesus spanned the chasm of sin to provide the way of our salvation.

When Jesus died on the cross he shouted, "It is finished!" (John 19:30). He didn't say, "I am finished." The fact was; he was far from finished. He arose on the third day and lives on in power today. What did he mean when he said, "It is finished?" He meant the bridge was finished. The way to God is now open. So clearly did the early Christians believe that Jesus was the way; they were commonly called "followers of the way."

But you ask, "How do I know this is true?" You must look at the evidence. This is what Jesus told John the Baptist.

John the Baptist had boldly declared about Jesus, "Look, the Lamb of God, who takes away the sin of the world!" (John 1:29). But in time John insulted King Herod and was cast into prison. Confined to a dungeon, he began to wonder if Jesus was really the Christ. Confinement can do that to you. Confinement in a jail, in a hospital room, or in a nursing home can cause you to doubt things you once affirmed.

John became unsure that Jesus was the Messiah. So he sent two of his servants to ask Jesus, "Are you the one who was to come, or should we expect someone else?" (Matthew 11:3).

Jesus told the servants to go and tell John again the things they had heard and seen: "The blind receive sight, the lame walk, those who have leprosy are cured, the deaf hear, the dead are raised, and the good news is preached to the poor" (Matthew 11:5).

Jesus could have easily given John the simple answer of "Yes, I am the Messiah." But instead, he instructed the men to tell John what he was doing. It was as if Jesus was saying, "Once John knows what I am doing, he will know who I am." Or to put it another way, Jesus was saying, "The proof is in the pudding." Once John examines the evidence he will know the answer to his question.

How then can we today be sure that Jesus is the Christ? How do we know that Christianity is superior to other religions? If you want to examine the evidence, then I suggest you do three things:

> Buy a book.
> Take a trip.
> Breathe a prayer.

What You Find in Christianity

First, if you want to know if Christianity is superior to other religions, buy a book.

Make a study of comparative religions and you'll discover the uniqueness of Christianity. What is unique? Listen to the testimony of the great Indian evangelist, Sundar Singh. He was reared as a Brahmin, but was never satisfied somehow with Brahminism—in spite of all that his father and family did to encourage him in this area. He was constantly searching in his younger days for reality and finally he found it in Jesus Christ.

Then he traveled all over the world as a great evangelistic influence for Christ. When asked what he found in Christianity that he did not find in any of the Eastern religions, he said, "What I found in Christianity was Christ."

In this respect Christianity is absolutely unique; it has Christ.

Who was Jesus? No man who has ever walked across the pages of human history has equaled the influence of Christ. He must be listed among the world's greatest figures. His personality, in unsurpassed splendor, has passed through the world and has altered the entire course of all subsequent history. The world has never been the same since Jesus came into it. That can't be denied by anyone who is honest.

His teachings have never been equaled in the annals of time. They tower above the works of other men like the mighty mountains tower above the oceans. They have impacted art and science and literature unlike anyone else who ever lived. From the day he walked the shores of Galilee and the dusty roads of Judea, men have heard in his voice the voice of God. It is safe to say, "Never a man so spoke."

Who then is he? Jesus demands an explanation. Some people say, "I'm prepared to accept him as a great teacher but not as God." That alternative is not open to us. Jesus made claims that force us to choose sides. He said, "I and the Father are one" (John 10:30) and "Anyone who has seen me has seen the Father" (John 14:9). He claimed to be God.

Either Jesus is who he said he is, or else he is an ego-maniac or a deceiver and a fraud. If he was deluded about himself, perhaps he was deluded about all else. If Jesus was deceived about himself, he may have been deceived about all else. A man who goes around claiming to be God must be God, or he is either deceptive or disillusioned. He is either God or a great imposter.

So we must accept Jesus for who he is, or reject him as deluded or deceptive. If we do the latter we are still faced with his influence on man. Jesus has accomplished more good for mankind than anyone else who has ever lived. If his claims are false, a lie has accomplished more good than the truth.

If you do not accept Jesus as Lord, you are compelled to explain the most unique life ever lived in some other way. You cannot be neutral about Jesus. You must accept him or write him off.

Jesus claims to forgive sins. That's quite silly and funny if he's not God. His enemies did not write him off as a fool. They took him seriously enough to crucify him. To accept him as a great teacher and not to accept his claims to be God is sheer foolishness. It is patronizing nonsense.

We contend that Jesus is the Son of God. All manmade religions consist chiefly of set teachings, formulas for living, and principles of conduct. Many believe that the central significance of Jesus is that he gave us moral instructions. But that is not true. If it were, the incarnation and atonement would be unnecessary, for there was no inadequacy in the Old Testament laws. If God spoke to Moses, he could have spoken again to expand, update, and clarify his law.

The Bible could have ended with Malachi. It would not have been necessary for Jesus to come and die. But it was not God's law (teaching) that was inadequate and needed improvement. It was man. Man was lost and could not save himself. Man had no power to keep the law. So the significance of Jesus is not just in what he taught; but who he was, and what he did. (Acts 1:1–3)

How can we know that Jesus is the Son of God? The resurrection provides proof. This is the sign he promised and guaranteed (Act 17:1–4, 31). How do I know that the resurrection occurred? The fact seems as secure as historical evidence can make it. We have the authority of history and the biblical witness to substantiate it.

Believing things on the authority of eyewitness accounts only means believing them because you have been told of them by someone you think is trustworthy. Most of what we believe, we believe on authority. I believe there is a place called Moscow in Russia. I have never seen it myself. I could not prove by abstract reasoning that there is such a place. I believe it because reliable people have told me so.

The ordinary man believes in the solar system, atoms, and the circulation of blood based on authority; because the scientists say so. Every historical statement in the world is believed on authority. None of us saw the Civil War or the American Revolution. None of us could prove them by pure logic as you prove a thing in mathematics. We believe them simply because people who did see them left writings that tell us about them. If a man scorned authority and other things as some people do with Christianity, then we would have no content to know anything at all about his life.

The evidence is in. Who can refute it? If the resurrection is true, then Christ is the Son of God.

If he is the Son of God, then Christianity is unique.

▬ Shopping in the Marketplace ▬ of World Religions

Second, to know that Christianity is unique, take a trip.

Take the advice of the old Quaker, "If thee would study comparative religions, don't buy a book, buy a ticket." Take a journey into lands where the influence of Christ has not yet penetrated.

Measure by performance and you will discover that Christianity has no equal. As F.J. Forakes-Jackson said, "History shows that Christ on the cross has been more potent than anything else in arousing a compassion for suffering and indignation at injustice."[3] It is Christ, more than anyone else, who exalts in us a compassion for the poor and needy.

It is easy for us to lose sight of the powerful influence of Christ upon the past twenty centuries. We are prone to take all good things for granted, as though they have always been here; or to think they came out of natural endowment. It is easy for us to forget how enormously Christ has changed the mental, moral, and social climate of the ages. How vastly different history would be if you tried to rewrite it without Christ.

Consider what Jesus has done for children. The world was hard before it was touched by Christian concern for the weak and the helpless. Among the Greeks, life was unbelievably cheap. Cheap in every stage of life. Babies were often not permitted to live. If the child was a male, healthy, and wanted; it was kept. If for any reason a child was not wanted, it was disposed of; left to die. It was a common practice.

Into the world came Christians. They counted all life as precious to God. They rescued the unwanted babies the pagans had thrown away and cared for them in the Christian community. Soon babies were left at the doorsteps of Christian homes instead of being thrown in the river. In time, public conscience quickened and laws were passed to prohibit child murder and exposure.

It was the same with women, slaves, and education. In colonial America, if you didn't want a *Christian* education, you didn't get any. All education was Christian. All colleges—Harvard first then Yale, Dartmouth, Princeton; and for a long time after, most institutions of higher learning were Christian. Even now, about one-third of colleges and universities are church-related and church-sponsored.

No other religion can boast such a record. In part such social concern is strangely lacking from most world religions. These are Christ's victories.

Phillip Yancey, in a *Christianity Today* article from 1997, pointed out even more examples of what I am talking about. He mentioned the modern hospice movement. Dame Ciecely Saunders, who founded the movement, was serving at St. Christopher's Hospital in London. A social worker and a nurse, she was appalled at the way medical staff treated people who were about to die—in essence, ignoring them as tokens of failure. This attitude offended her as a Christian, for she knew that care for the dying was traditionally one of the church's seven works of mercy.

Since no one would listen to a nurse, she returned to medical school in middle age and became a doctor. She then founded a place where people could come to die with dignity and without pain. Now there are more than 4,700 hospice houses in the United States.

Think of the thousands of chapters of Alcoholics Anonymous that meet in church basements, VFW halls, and living rooms all across the nation every night of the week. Christians who founded Alcoholics Anonymous faced the choice of whether to make it a restrictively Christian organization or to found it on Christian principles and then set it free. They chose the latter. The recovery model is based on dependence on a "higher power" and a supportive community—a lifeline against addiction to alcohol, drugs, sex, and food.

Or consider Millard Fuller, a millionaire entrepreneur who was rich and miserable, with his marriage on the rocks. He came under the spell of Clarence Jordan, a radical Christian, who helped him. Fuller gave away his personal fortune and founded an organization on the simple premise that every person on the planet deserved a decent place to live. Today, Habitat for Humanity organizes hundreds of thousands of volunteers and they have built over 5,280 homes for the underprivileged.

Another example is the Salvation Army. It was founded by Methodist minister William Booth to care for the downtrodden poor in the slums of London, England. In time it spread to a world-wide ministry. Its motto: "Soup! Soap! And Salvation—fill 'em up, clean 'em up and lift 'em up" is more than a slogan. It is the daily salvation for millions of people the world over.

Then add Prison Fellowship, founded by Chuck Colson, former president Richard Nixon's hatchet man; who was imprisoned himself for his part in the Watergate scandal. In prison he became a Christian and upon his release devoted his life to rehabilitating ex-convicts into society as followers of Christ and productive citizens.

On and on the list could go. If you were shopping at the marketplace of world religions, your best buy would be Christianity. Measured by its performance, there is no other religion with a record that approaches it.

Based on this record it is safe to say that if Christianity is not true, we must admit that a lie has accomplished more than good than the truth has. Can you think of another area where this is true? It's not possible.

Give it a try.

▬ From Beer to Furniture ▬

Third, breathe a prayer.

Bow your head and your heart and put your faith and trust in Jesus.

That's the ultimate test. Christianity is the only religion that offers power. It not only tells us what is right, it enables us to do it. It not only provides moral insight, but moral power. This is man's greatest need.

Christ is not just a sage. He is the Savior.

This is more than a mere claim. It has been demonstrated as a fact in everyday experience right down through the centuries. For those who wholeheartedly put their faith in Christ, who really commit their lives to Christ, these things have happened.

Here is a distinctive claim for Christ. When Christianity loses its power to convert, to relate, and to transform character, it will lose its right to be called Christianity.

To me, the strongest proof that Jesus is the Christ, and the Son of God who came to earth with the power to save me, is not what happened when he was on earth. Rather it is because of what he does for people today.

There was a man who struggled with alcoholism off and on for many years. When he was dry, he cared for his family, bought furniture for the house, paid the rent, and did as a father should. But when he started drinking again he would sell the furniture piece by piece to buy liquor and squander his money on beer. Then he became a Christian. One day a friend sneeringly said to him, "You don't really believe that yarn about Jesus turning water into wine?"

The new convert replied, "I am an uneducated man. I don't know about water and wine. But I know this, Jesus came into my life and he has turned beer into furniture! And that's a good enough miracle for me."

C.S. Lewis, the great Christian apologist was once an atheist. He wrote after his conversion, "I believe in Christianity as I believe that the sun has risen. Not only because I see it, but because by it I see everything else."[4]

Through faith in Christ I see myself, the world, and eternity as they really are; and life makes sense for the first time. The question is, "Will you trust him?" Jesus said, "If anyone chooses to do God's will, he will find out whether my teaching comes from God or whether I speak on my own" (John 7:17).

You need only to bow your head and your heart before Christ, not for what you'll get out of him, but because of who he is. No other reason is needed or sufficient.

On one occasion Jesus preached a hard sermon and afterward saw many of his followers go away. He then asked his disciples, "'You do not want to leave too, do you?' Jesus asked the Twelve. Simon Peter answered him, 'Lord, to whom shall we go? You have the words of eternal life'" (John 6:67–68).

If Christianity is not the truth of God, where else can we go? To Muhammad? To Buddha? To Confucius?

We must either swim with Jesus or sink in despair.

Jesus comes saying simply, "Follow me and you'll know from experience that I speak the truth."

Will you follow him?

─────────────── N O T E S ───────────────

1. *Tyler Morning Telegraph*, December 25, 2010.

2. *The Confessions of St. Augustine, Bishop of Hippo*, Book 1, Chapter 1.

3. F.J. Forakes-Jackson, "Christ in the Church: The Testimony of History" in *Essays on Some Theological Questions of the Day*, Henry Barclay Swete, ed. (London: Macmillan and Company, 1906), 513.

4. C.S. Lewis, *The Weight of Glory: And Other Addresses* (New York, NY: HarperCollins Publishers, 2001 [original copyright 1949]), 140.

6

Coming to God

When he came to his senses, he said, "How many of my father's hired men have food to spare, and here I am starving to death! I will set out and go back to my father and say to him: Father, I have sinned against heaven and against you."

Luke 15:17–18

I became a follower of Christ when I was fourteen-years-of-age. I don't think there has been a day since then, when I would have ever said, "I do not want to follow Christ." But I did not always follow as closely or as obediently as I could have. Sometimes I lagged behind and he had to wait for me to catch up. Sometimes I wandered off the trail and he had to send someone or something to call me back. But in these latter years I am more and more grateful that I always came back home.

Whether as an individual or a church, we need to ask ourselves if we need to repent. Do we need to turn from the way we are living and what we are doing; and return to God?

What do churches need to repent of? Some have forsaken their first love like the church in Ephesus (Revelation 2:4). Some have lost their passion, that sense of loyalty that characterized them when they were first converted. Now they muddle through worship, don't sing with gusto, don't listen with intensity, and leave thinking as they did in the days of Malachi, "What a burden!" (Malachi 1:13).

Some churches tolerate false teachers and false teachings as did the churches in Pergamum and Thyatira

(Revelation 2:12–29). False teachings are like leaven in a lump of dough. They soon spread throughout the whole congregation.

Some churches are dead like Sardis (Revelation 3:1). They are an unburied corpse. Committees continue to meet. The budget is balanced. The buildings are clean. But there is no life, vitality, or enthusiasm. No one is being saved and people are not growing in Christ's likeness.

And some are like the church at Laodicea (Revelation 3:14–22). They are proud and self-sufficient. They say to themselves, "'We are rich; we have acquired wealth and do not need a thing.' But they do not realize that they are wretched, pitiful, poor, blind and naked" before God.

In the story of the Prodigal Son, Jesus gives us an illustration of the path back home to God. Luke begins by telling us that publicans and sinners (people of doubtful reputation) were being attracted to Jesus. The Pharisees and the Scribes complained that he treated these people like they were his friends. In response to their criticism, Jesus told three parables that contrasted their attitude with the heart of God.

First Jesus told of a man who had a hundred sheep. Ninety-nine of them were safe in the fold but one was lost. Sheep can easily become lost. They nibble a little here and there and the first thing they know, they are lost.

He left the ninety-nine and searched until he found the one that was lost. When he found him, he laid him across his shoulders and when he returned home he called his friends together and they rejoiced with him over the lost sheep that had been found.

Then Jesus said, "I tell you that in the same way there will be more rejoicing in heaven over one sinner who repents than over ninety-nine righteous persons who do not need to repent" (Luke 15:7).

Next Jesus told the parable of a woman who had ten coins. She accidentally dropped one of them on the floor. The Palestinian houses were very dark, with only a small opening for a window. The floor was beaten earth covered with dried reeds and rushes. To look for a coin on a floor like that was very much like looking for a needle in a haystack. The coin in question was a silver drachma which was equivalent to a whole day's wage for a working man. So she diligently swept the floor hoping that she might see the coin glint, or hear it tinkle as it moved among the rushes.

When she found it, she called her friends together and they rejoiced with her. Then Jesus added this comment, "In the same way, I tell you, there is rejoicing in the presence of the angels of God over one sinner who repents" (Luke 15:10).

Then Jesus told the story of the Prodigal Son or perhaps the story of the Loving Father. It is the greatest short story ever told.

It simply begins, "A certain man had two sons . . ." (Luke 15:11, KJV). Obviously the youngest son and his father had had a conflict of wills. So the son said to his father, "Give me my part of the family inheritance and I'm out of your house and out of your hair forever."

Under Jewish law a father was free to leave his property when he liked, but not as he liked. The eldest son was to receive two-thirds of the inheritance, and the younger son one-third (Deuteronomy 21:17). It was by no means unusual for a father to distribute his estate before he died, especially if he wished to retire from the actual management of his affairs.

So, not many days after that, the younger son packed his bags with everything he had because he did not intend to come back home. Then he took a trip into the far country.

The "far country" is not a *geographical location* but a *spiritual condition*. You can live next door to the church and be in the far country. You can grow up in a parsonage and be in the far country. The far country is any place away from God.

Away from his father's house, the young man wasted his inheritance in wild, loud living. In no time he had spent all his father had taken a lifetime to accumulate. Unable to find other work, the younger son wound up feeding pigs, a task that was an abomination to Jews. It was the deepest kind of humility. In today's culture it would be equivalent to living on the streets and eating out of a dumpster.

In this miserable condition, "he came to himself," (i.e., came to his senses.) He said in essence, "I've played the fool. I've made a mess out of life. I got my way and it got me nowhere. My father's servants are faring better than I. They have three square meals a day and a roof over their head and I have nothing."

Then he resolved, "I am going back home and say to my father, "Father, I have sinned against heaven and before you and I'm not worthy to be called your son; make me as one of your hired servants." For the younger son, the three hardest three words for him to say were, "I have sinned." It is the same for us.

The younger son left home saying, "give me" with the intent of never returning home. He returned home saying, "make me one of your hired help." He didn't stop with a resolution. He moved. He got up and headed for home. That's repentance. That's coming back to God.

When he was a great way off, his father saw him and ran to meet him. This is the only place in the Bible where God is ever pictured as being in a hurry. He threw his arms around the neck of his boy, kissed him, and welcomed him home. The boy had been out of his house but not out of his heart. That's the great heart of God.

The father quickly told the servants, "Go and get some clean clothes for my boy. Put some shoes on his feet. Put the family ring back on his finger. Kill one of our finest calves and prepare a feast so we can celebrate. For this my son was dead and is alive again; was lost and is found." And they began to celebrate.

This is a perfect picture of repentance. First the boy came to himself; then he came to the father; then he came clean. Real repentance involves all three of these steps. But remember, there were two sons.

The older son never did any of the immoral things his younger brother did. He stayed home, lived by the rules of his Father, and helped with the work around the farm. But when he heard that his wayward brother had come back home and was being celebrated by the family; he became angry and jealous. He wouldn't even go to the party.

Though his father begged him to come in, he would not. He said to his father, "All of these years I served you, I never disobeyed you at any time, and you never had a party for me and my friends. But as soon as your son, who wasted everything you earned with prostitutes, came back home; you had a celebration for him."

Notice that he referred to his brother as "your son" not "my brother." Obviously he had no sorrow at his brother's leaving and no joy at his return.

The father tried to reassure the older son that all that he had was his. He tried to persuade him that it was fitting they should rejoice at the return of his brother. But the older brother would have none of it. He had lived in his father's house all his life, but had never learned what brought joy to his father's heart.

The elder brother represented the Pharisees and their self-righteous, judgmental, and unloving attitude toward the publicans and sinners who were coming to Christ. This attitude was the exact opposite of that exhibited by Jesus.

Both boys needed repentance. One needed forgiveness for what he had done; the other for what he had become. One needed to repent for his actions; and the other for his attitude. One's sin was of the flesh; the other's was a sin of the spirit. One was rebellious; the other was resentful. Both were sinners and both needed repentance.

The boys represent all of us. Like the Prodigal Son we may need forgiveness for what we have done. Like the elder brother we may need forgiveness for what we are. We may need to repent of immoral living or we may need to repent of a critical, judgmental, and unloving spirit toward others.

In either case this beautiful story shows us the way back home. We must take the steps that the Prodigal Son took if we are to be made right with God.

> We must come to ourselves.
> We must come to the Father.
> We must come clean.

▬ Re-examining Our Assumptions ▬

First, we must come to ourselves.

Like the Prodigal Son we must come to our senses and realize we have made wrong choices. We must admit, as he did, that the far country was a far cry from what he had expected. *We have to be fed up with being fed what the world has to offer.*

As long as you are happy in the hog pen you will never leave it for the Father's house.

Repentance always involves regret, admitting to yourself and to God your sorrow. There can be repentance without tears, but there can be no repentance without regret, sorrow, and grief. Sin embarrasses and humiliates the sinner. But not everyone cries.

Jonah preached to the people of Nineveh concerning their wicked life. The text states, "The Ninevites believed God. They declared a fast, and all of them, from the greatest to the least, put on sackcloth. When the news reached the king of Nineveh, he rose from his throne, took off his royal robes, covered himself with sackcloth and sat down in the dust" (Jonah 3:5–6).

That's repentance.

Charles Haddon Spurgeon expressed it this way in a poem:

> Repentance is to leave
> The sins we loved before,
> And show that we in earnest grieve,
> By doing so no more.[1]

Merle Miller in his book on the life of Lyndon Johnson entitled, *Lyndon, an Oral Biography* quoted him concerning the U.S. involvement in the Vietnam War, "I never felt that I had the luxury of re-examining my basic assumptions. Once the decision to commit military force was made, all our energies were turned to vindicating that choice and finding a way to make it work."[2]

If we never take time to re-examine our basic assumptions we may find ourselves forever lost. We need to ask ourselves honestly, "Am I going in the right direction? Have I made the right decision? Have I moved away from the Father?" We must not alibi or try to justify. We've got to face the fact of our failure.

▬ God Permits U-Turns ▬

Second, we must come to the Father.

It is not enough to realize you have made a mistake, or to regret what you have done, or even to resolve to do better. You must return to God. You must act. You must get up and come to him.

If you find yourself going in the wrong direction in your car it doesn't do any good to beat on the steering wheel or get irritated at your wife. It is not her fault. And it won't help to stomp on the accelerator and go faster. You need to admit your mistake, at least to yourself, turn around, and start going in the right direction. That's repentance.

Jesus told another story about a man who had two sons (Matthew 21:28–32) and he came to the first and said, "Go work today in my vineyard." And the boy answered and said, "I will not." But afterwards he repented and went.

He came to his second son and said the same thing. He answered his Father and said, "I go, sir." But he didn't go.

Then Jesus asked, "Which of the two did the will of his father?" The answer is obvious: the one who surrendered his will to the will of his father. Returning to God means that we surrender our will to his will. It is turning from rebellion to obedience. That's repentance.

▬ Rummaging Through the Suitcase ▬

Third, we must come clean.

The Prodigal Son went to his father and confessed, "Father, I have sinned against heaven and against you. I am no longer worthy to be called your son" (Luke 15:21). He came to himself, came to his father, and came clean. That's what we must do.

"I've sinned against heaven." All sin is against God. It may hurt others but it is primarily against God. Repentance involves confession of that. Frederick Buechner reminds us, "to confess your sins to God is not telling him anything he doesn't already know. Until you confess them, however, they are an abyss between you. When you confess them, they become the Golden Gate Bridge."[3]

Someone has said, "Sin is like a seed . . . to cover it is to cultivate it." The Scriptures say the same thing. "He that covereth his sin shall not prosper, but he that confesseth and forsaketh his sin shall find mercy" (Proverbs 28:13, KJV). We must confess it and we must forsake it. Admit it and quit it.

Years ago I hired a professor to teach at Truett Seminary who had a checkered past. He had at one time been the bright and shining star of Baptist preachers and had climbed the pinnacle of success. Unfortunately, (and by his own admission) ambition got the better of him.

He was soon out of the church, divorced from his wife, and on the streets as a door-to-door salesman. For several years he did not preach. It was a wilderness experience during which he humbled himself and got right with God.

In time, black churches began to invite him to preach in their pulpits.

We had been longtime friends and I invited him to speak in our chapel to test the reaction of my faculty. They liked what they heard. I then invited him to preach at our pastor's conference to see the reaction of the pastors. They loved him. I then invited him to teach an I-term course to see how the administration would react. They were favorable. I then presented him to our faculty as a prospective faculty member.

Before a faculty member is appointed, they meet with the other faculty members of the department and must receive a recommendation from them. So we gathered one day in a conference room and I began by saying, "Friend, you bring a lot of baggage to this job. We are going to open the suitcase and rummage through it. No holds barred."

So for almost an hour our faculty questioned him about his past life, and in particular, his present commitment to the Lord. When we were through he said, "What I did was not just a mistake, it was a sin against God. And I have sought and found the forgiveness of the Lord."

With that, our faculty affirmed him and their affirmation has proven to be justified.

What we did that day you must do with God. You must open your suitcase and rummage through it, pulling up all the dirty laundry and letting God wash it clean.

When we come in a spirit of humility and repentance, he welcomes us home. God doesn't expect us to be perfect, but he does expect us to be perfectly honest.

Jesus, on another occasion, told the story of a rich man who lived a life of luxury and ease (Luke 16:19–31). A beggar named Lazarus sat outside his gate and willingly ate scraps from the man's garbage can. In time the beggar died and went to heaven.

The rich man died and went to hell.

In hell, he cried out to Abraham asking that the beggar dip the tip of his finger in water and cool his parched lips. Abraham responded that that was impossible. There was a gulf between them that could not be crossed.

The man, realizing his fate was forever settled, asked that Lazarus be sent to his family's house to warn them lest they make the same mistake that he had made, and come to that place of torment.

Abraham answered and said, "They have preachers and the Bible. Let them hear them." And the man responded, "Yes but if one returns from the dead they would listen and they would repent."

And when he said, "they would repent" he was admitting that was what he should have done. That was what he needed.

And that is the need of every life. Jesus warns, "But unless you repent, you too will all perish" (Luke 13:3).

Our only hope is to turn to God.

The good news is:
God permits u-turns.

NOTES

1. http://www.spurgeon.org/sermons/0460.htm. Accessed 5/22/2014.

2. Merle Miller, *Lyndon: An Oral Biography* (New York, NY: Ballantine Books, 1981).

3. Frederick Beuchner, *Wishful Thinking: A Seeker's ABC* (New York: HarperOne, 1973, 1993), 18.

Preaching at Green Acres Baptist Church.
Served as Pastor from 1972-1989.

BAPTIST STANDARD

November 12, 1986

New BGCT Officers Elected for 1987

Officers elected last week at the 101st annual meeting of the Baptist General Convention of Texas were (l-r) President Paul Powell, pastor of Green Acres Church, Tyler; First Vice President David Benitez, pastor of Hispana Church, El Paso; Second Vice President Joe E. Briscoe, from First Church, Devine. (Kendall Kirk Photo)

Served as President of the
Baptist General Convention of Texas in 1987.

Paul and Cathy Powell.

Paul, Cathy, and their children:
Kent Powell, Lori Powell Gropper, and Mike Powell.

THE YEARS AHEAD

Annuity Board of the Southern Baptist Convention
Summer 1990

ANNUITY BOARD POISED FOR THE NEW DECADE

STEWARDSHIP — GOING BEYOND MONEY

President of the Annuity Board of the
Southern Baptist Convention (1989-1998).

BUT HE'S STILL A MINISTER
— Annuity Board President Paul W. Powell

Playing golf at Augusta National Golf Club (1998).

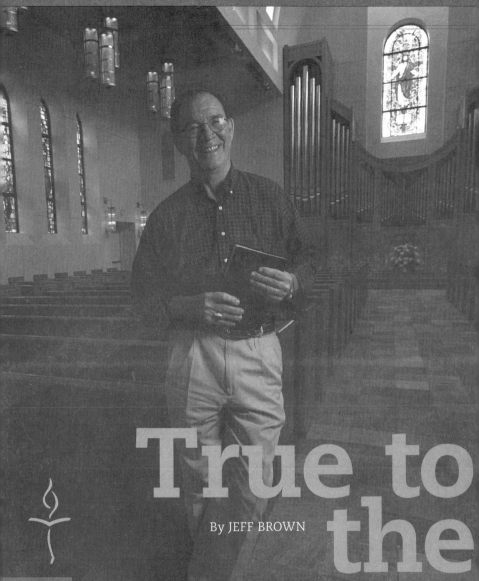

True to the

By JEFF BROWN

sion is to be the premier
ological seminary in the
ormer Dean Paul Powell,
n the seminary's chapel,
which bears his name.

A decade after its first graduating class and over a
century after its namesake helped save Baylor University,
George W. Truett Theological Seminary remains
committed to preparing ministers and missionaries for
worldwide Christian service.

Dean, George W. Truett Theological Seminary (2001-2007).
Standing in chapel named in his honor.

Dedication of Truett Seminary Campus with
Sysco Corporation founder and Baptist benefactor
John Baugh, and his wife Eula Mae Baugh.

Working with Cowboy Churches.
Ft. Worth, Texas (2008).

Led prayer at the opening of the United States Congress (June 29, 2010). From left to right: Chaplain of the House Fr. Daniel Coughlin, daughter Lori Powell Gropper, grandson Matthew Gropper, wife Cathy, and U.S. Representative Louie Gohmert.

Great Honor

...ler Resident Powell Receives Exemplary Service Medal

Commencement Speaker at
San Marcos Baptist Academy (2011).

7

Thanking God

For as high as the heavens are above the earth, so great is his love for those who fear him; as far as the east is from the west, so far has he removed our transgressions from us. As a father has compassion on his children, so the LORD has compassion on those who fear him.

Psalm 103:11–13

For a large part of my life I took things—my family, my friends, my health, my calling—for granted. As I've grown older I have learned to be more grateful for these things. And I now try to make every day a day of thanks and giving.

In Kirk Douglas' autobiography, *The Ragman's Son*, he tells of a trip to Pakistan in the early 1980s; a time of Communist aggression in that area. He met with some refugees from Afghanistan near Khyber Pass. Douglas sat on the ground with the elders around the fire. They ate with their fingers out of a common bowl. To an interpreter, Douglas told the Afghan leaders: "In my country, today is Thanksgiving Day, one day every year that we set aside to give thanks for all that we have in life."

The leader of the elders, a man with a long, white beard, responded through an interpreter, "In my country, we give thanks every day."[1]

All of us, like Kirk Douglas, need to be reminded that every day is Thanksgiving Day. That story carried me back to Douglas' beginnings. He was born in Amsterdam, New York, the son of an illiterate, Russian Jew. His name was Issur Danielovitch, later changed to Izzy Demsky. His father collected and sold rags for a living but was drunk most of the time.

Douglas said on good days, he and his six sisters and his mother ate eggs scrambled with water for dinner while his father, the ragman, was off on a drunk. On bad days, they didn't eat.

Even on Eagle Street, he writes, "In the poorest section of town, where all the families were struggling, the ragman was the lowest rung on the ladder. And I was the ragman's son."[2]

As he grew older, he began to attend the American Academy of Dramatic Arts on a scholarship, wearing a cast-off coat that was so long it swept the streets. At night he waited tables at Schrafft's, stuffing leftover sandwiches in his mouth. On Thanksgiving Day, he waited in line at the Salvation Army for a meal.

Douglas, like many of us, knew what it was like to have little; and then later to have much. That is all the more reason for us to make every day Thanksgiving Day. I'm not talking about turkey and dressing and pumpkin pie. I'm talking about things more basic than that.

My old professor at Baylor University, Kyle Yates, said of Psalm 103, "It is the most beautiful, most perfect, most comprehensive of all the psalms of thanksgiving." Look at it with me.

The psalmist begins, "Bless the Lord, O my soul; and all that is within me, bless his holy name. Bless the Lord, O my soul, and forget not all his benefits . . ." (Psalm 103:1, KJV)

The word "bless" comes from a root word meaning "to kneel." It suggests bowing before God in praise and thanksgiving. We are to do it with "all that is within us," i.e., from head to toe.

The danger, as the psalmist points out, is that we will "forget" all his benefits.

Then the writer lists five reasons for our thankfulness. God has forgiven our sins; he heals us of our diseases; he saves us from destruction; he crowns our lives with loving kindness and tender mercies; and finally; he satisfies us with good things.

In this chapter I want to focus on verses 11–13 where the psalmist teaches us about God's mercies by using the literary tool of comparison. These verses speak of the heights of God's love, the breadth of God's love, and the depth of God's love. It is teaching by comparison.

These are the things for which we should be grateful:

) God's unending mercy.
) God's unlimited forgiveness.
) God's unconditional love.

▬ How High Is the Sky? ▬

First, we should thank God for his unending mercy.

The word mercy is better translated, "goodness" or "kindness." The psalmist says that as the heavens are higher than the earth, so great is God's goodness and kindness to us.

When the psalmist wrote those words he had no idea how high heaven was above the earth. Come to think of it, neither do we. But, let me try to explain it this way: light travels at the speed of 186,000 miles per second. At that speed it can encircle the globe seven times every second. That's not as fast as my wife drives, but it's pretty fast.

In two seconds traveling at that speed, we pass the moon. In eight-and-a-half minutes we pass the sun, which is 96,000,000 miles away. In five years we come to the end of the Solar System which is made of the sun and eight planets. (Poor Pluto; downgraded from a planet to a comet.) In 4.5 trillion years (not seconds, not hours, not days, not months, but years), traveling at the speed of light, we come to the part of the universe that telescopes are unable to reach.

What else is there beyond the veil of darkness? If we could get to the end of space, what would be on the other side? We cannot imagine space without end, but everything we know says that it is the truth.

So, how high is the heaven above the earth? It is unending. That is how great God's kindness and goodness is to us.

William Wilberforce was a great British reformer. More than anyone else, he was responsible for the eradication of the slave trade in the British Empire. He inherited a fortune from his uncle and would not have had to work at all in his life. But he decided to devote his life to public service.

He entered Parliament in 1780 at the age of twenty-four. In those days he was skeptical of religion and often ridiculed the Christian faith. Then, through the witness of a former tutor, he began a serious search for God.

He had long admired John Newton, who was the pastor of a church in Olney. Newton had written the great hymn, "Amazing Grace."

Before his conversion, Newton had been the captain of a slave ship. Caught in a terrible storm in 1749, he began a spiritual search that brought him to Christ.

Wilberforce asked for an appointment with Newton to discuss his spiritual life. When the time came, he walked around Newton's house two or three times trying to decide if he would go in. After all Wilberforce was a member of Parliament, and his conversion to Christianity would immediately become news.

In 1786, at the age of thirty, Wilberforce became a follower of Christ. He considered going into the ministry, but Newton urged him to stay in the political arena and to use his platform there as a way to change the world. He pointed him to the Old Testament hero Daniel as one who served God through government.

Shortly after his conversion, Wilberforce said that the Lord had set before him two great objectives—the suppression of the slave trade in the British Empire and the reformation of "manners" (the old English word for "morals"). He immediately set himself to the task. Every year for twenty years he made a motion and a passionate plea before Parliament that slavery be abolished. And, every year for twenty years he was voted down. He was cursed, threatened, and challenged to duels countless times because of his moral stand.

Wilberforce retired from Parliament without slavery having been abolished. But it remained on the hearts and minds of the members, and two days before he died, Parliament voted to outlaw slavery in the British Empire. It was a momentous event for the entire world.

After retirement, Wilberforce gave himself to all manner of good causes. One biographer said of him, "Good causes stuck to him like pins to a magnet."[3]

With the help of friends, Wilberforce established soup kitchens, lending libraries, and schools for the poor, the deaf, and the blind. He sponsored small pox vaccinations, and worked for shorter working hours and better working conditions in factories. He went into prisons, funded and established hospitals, and purchased the freedom of those in prison for debt.

Wilberforce also helped found The Royal Society for the Prevention of Cruelty to Animals and The National Gallery. He wrote books and magazines and distributed Bibles around the world. He sought more humane treatment for Native Americans and for the people of India. And he paid tuition for students to go to college. There was no good cause beyond his interest and concern.

In his later years Wilberforce faced many difficulties. He lost much of his wealth. He gave twenty-five percent of it to charity. He loaned money to friends that was never repaid and he made some poor investments. He had four children: three sons and a daughter. Two of his sons became ministers but one was a drunkard and a liar. His only daughter died, and he was chronically ill for many years.

At the age of seventy-four, Wilberforce wrote, "I can scarcely understand why my life has been spared so long except to show that a man can be happy without a fortune as well as with one."[4] His son, Samuel, said the chief feature of his father's life in his later years was gratitude. One phrase conveyed it best, "How good a friend God has been to me."

Can't we all say that? If you ask me for a one sentence testimony it would be, "How good a friend God is to me." I can adopt the declaration of David that "goodness and mercy have followed me all the days of my life" (Ps. 23:6a, KJV).

I know of God's unending kindness and goodness.

▬ If We Deserved It, It Wouldn't Be Mercy ▬

Second, we should give thanks for God's unlimited forgiveness.

The psalmist said, "as far as the east is from the west, so far has he removed our transgressions from us" (Ps. 103:12).

How far is the east from the west? It is limitless. It is significant that the psalmist did not say, "As far as the north is from the south, so far hath he removed our transgressions from us." That's because there is a limit to both the northern and southern directions. Begin where you are and travel northward and eventually you come to the North Pole. Once you pass it you are no longer traveling north, you are traveling south. Travel far enough south and you will eventually come to the South Pole. Once you pass it you are no longer traveling south, you are traveling north. There is a limit to how far you can travel to the north or to the south.

But, there is no east pole or west pole. Begin traveling east and you can encircle the globe endlessly and you will always be traveling east. There is no limit to the east or to the west. That's how far God has removed our sins from us.

Remember who wrote this psalm. It was David, the king of Israel. He was a man after God's own heart. God had chosen him, anointed him as king, and blessed him immeasurably. But at mid-life David fell in love with another man's wife and had an adulterous relationship with her.

Soon Bathsheba realized she was pregnant (2 Samuel 11).

Clearly the baby was not her husband's because he was on the battlefield fighting in Israel's army. Obviously abortion was not an option, so what were they to do to cover up their sin? David had an idea. He would bring her husband home for rest and recuperation; the husband would sleep with his wife, and would then think that the child was his.

David's plot was foiled when Uriah, her husband, returned home but refused the comfort of his own home as long as his fellow soldiers were on the battlefield.

Then David devised another plan. Through his general Joab he would have Uriah sent to the front lines. Then he would give word to his fellow soldiers to retreat; leaving Uriah to face the enemy alone.

Just as David had planned, Uriah was killed and his sin was safely covered. Or was it? Other people did not know about it, but David knew about it and God knew about it; and it troubled David's soul. He was torn between the desire to conceal his sin and the need to reveal his sin. He confessed that by keeping silent he was growing old before his time. He lived under great inner pressure. And he was drying up on the inside. (Ps. 32:3–4)

Then he said, "I acknowledged my sin to you and did not cover up my iniquity. I said, 'I will confess my transgressions to the LORD'—and you forgave the guilt of my sin.'"(Ps. 32:5).

Then he declared, "Blessed is he whose transgressions are forgiven, whose sins are covered" (Ps. 32:1). David, who was guilty of adultery and murder, came to know from his own experience that God's forgiveness is limitless.

A young soldier in Napoleon's army deserted his post. He was tried, found guilty, and condemned to death. His mother went to the emperor to plead for her son. She asked the general to have mercy on him and forgive him.

The general replied, "Madam, your son does not deserve mercy."

And she responded, "O sir. If he deserved it, it would not be mercy."

The general replied, "You are right, and so he shall have mercy. He is forgiven."[5]

That's the unlimited forgiveness of God.

━ It's My Boy ━

Third, we need to give thanks for God's unconditional love.

The psalmist wrote, "Like a father pitieth his children, so the Lord pitieth them that fear him" (Ps. 103:13, KJV). The word pity is best translated "compassion, love." Like a father loves his child, so God loves us.

We see a picture of a compassionate father's love in the story of Dick and Rick Hoyt. Rick was born to Dick and Judy Holt in 1962. Due to some complications at birth, Rick was diagnosed as a spastic quadriplegic with cerebral palsy. The doctors counseled the Hoyt's to have Rick institutionalized, but they refused. They determined to provide him with as normal a life as possible.

When he was twelve, Rick was able to communicate with his parents through a speech device. He told them he wanted to participate in a fundraising run for a teen who had been paralyzed in an accident. Though not a runner, Dick agreed to push Rick's wheelchair in the race. When it was over, Rick told his dad, "Dad, when I'm running, it feels like I'm not handicapped."[6]

That was the beginning. For the past thirty-seven years Dick has pushed, pulled, and carried his son in thousands of races and the Hoyts have even competed in the Ironman triathlon. They recently completed their final Boston Marathon.

Rick graduated from Boston University and lives in his own apartment. He has proved that people with disabilities can accomplish amazing things, especially with the support of a loving family.

When Dick is praised as an inspiration, his response is, "I just love my family and I just want to be the very best father I can be."[7] Dick Hoyt has demonstrated unconditional love for his son in some marvelous ways. How great it is that we have a Heavenly Father who loves us unconditionally and wants us to be the very best that we have been created to be!

A man had a wayward son and a friend said to him on one occasion, "If that was my boy I'd let him go." He responded, "If he was your boy I would let him go too. But he's not your boy. He's mine. And I cannot let him go."

That's a father's unconditional love.

If all of this were not enough, the psalmist then says that our lives are but a brief moment compared to eternity. We are like grass that soon withers. We are like flowers that are soon blown away by the wind. But God's loving kindness is from everlasting to everlasting. It is unending, unlimited, and unconditional (Ps. 103:15–18).

I spoke of John Newton earlier. Late in life his eyesight failed him and as he dictated his memories to his secretary he said, "My memory is nearly gone, but I remember two things—that I am a great sinner, and that Christ is a great Saviour."[8]

It is the goodness of God that should lead us to repentance. (Romans 2:4) It is not our fear of God but rather our gratitude to God that should cause us to turn to him.

What a tragedy if in the face of all that goodness and grace we should be lost forever.

On Saturday, February 1, 2003, the space shuttle Columbia exploded over East Texas and all seven astronauts lost their lives. The next day the headlines in the *Dallas Morning News* read in big print, "Tragedy Over Texas."

The byline read, "Columbia lost sixteen minutes from home."

Think of it, almost home, but lost.

Don't let that happen to you.

Respond to the love, mercy, and goodness of God today.

NOTES

1. Kirk Douglas, *The Ragman's Son* (New York, NY: Simon & Schuster Inc. 1988), 420.

2. Ibid., 7.

3. Kevin Belmonte and Charles Colson, *William Wilberforce: A Hero for Humanity* (Grand Rapids, Michigan: Zondervan, 2002, 2007), 17.

4. Stoughton, John. 1882. "The Life of William Wilberforce." *The Friend: A Religious and Literary Journal* 40:37 (April 7): 291.

5. http://www.christianlibrary.org/authors/Grady_Scott/matt5-7.htm. Accessed 5/22/2014.

6. http://www.lifenews.com/2014/04/21/inspirational-father-son-team-dick-and-rick-hoyt-race-their-last-boston-marathon/. Accessed 5/29/2014.

7. Ibid.

8. http://www.wholesomewords.org/biography/bnewton4.html. Accessed 5/22/2014.

8

Trusting God

I was young and now I am old, yet I have never seen the righteous forsaken or their children begging bread.

Psalm 37:25

*A*t the age of sixty-nine, Ronald Reagan was the oldest man ever elected president of the United States. Prior to that, he was governor of California in the 1960s. Those were years of political and social turmoil, especially on college campuses.

Once a group of students came to his office and said: "Governor, we want to talk to you but we think you should realize that it's impossible for you to understand us . . . it's sad, but it's impossible for a member of your generation to understand your own children . . ."

"You weren't raised in a time of instant communication or satellites and computers solving problems in seconds that previously took hours or days or even weeks to solve. You didn't live in the day of space travel and journeys to the moon or jet travel or high speed electronics . . ."

When he paused to take his breath, Reagan answered, "You're absolutely right. We didn't have those when we were your age. We invented them . . ."[1]

During a question-and-answer period with students at Moscow (Russia) State University in 1988, Reagan told the young crowd, ". . . you're going to be surprised how much you recall the feelings you had in these days here and that—how easy it is to understand the young people (when you get older) because of your own having been young once. You know an awful lot more about being young than you do about being old."[2]

While there are things we may not understand about one another because of age differences, there are some things we must not misunderstand regardless of our age. One is the faithfulness of God. The psalmist testifies to this when he writes, "I was young and now I am old, yet I have never seen the righteous forsaken or their children begging bread." (Psalm 37:25)

God's mercy is everlasting. His promises are unfailing. He is faithful to care for his people in every generation. The truth of it can be seen in the lives of three senior citizens in the Bible—Caleb, Eli, and David.

> ⟩ Caleb teaches us God is faithful to get us through the wildernesses of life, if we will trust him.
> ⟩ Eli teaches us God is faithful to reveal his plan for our life, if we will listen to his voice.
> ⟩ David teaches us God is faithful to get us home safely at the end of life, if we will follow the shepherd.

▬ Cheerleaders for Progress ▬

First, Caleb teaches us God is faithful to get us through the wildernesses of life, if we trust him.

We first meet Caleb when Israel is eighteen months out of Egypt. God appears to Moses and says to him, "I have indeed seen the misery of my people in Egypt. I have heard them crying out because of their slave drivers, and I am concerned about their suffering. So I have come down to rescue them from the hand of the Egyptians and to bring them up out of that land into a good and spacious land, a land flowing with milk and honey" (Exodus 3:7–8).

That phrase, "a land flowing with milk and honey" is used twenty-one times to describe the Promised Land. It was the Lord's way of describing the wonder and plenty of the land he is taking them to. It is only an eleven-day journey by foot walking straight from Egypt to the land of Canaan. So the Israelites could have been there in less than two weeks. But God routed them into the Sinai Peninsula where they camped for a year at Mount Sinai. He gave them his law and shaped them into a nation.

Eighteen months out of Egypt they arrive at the border of the Promised Land. God instructs Moses to choose twelve spies (one from each of the twelve tribes) and to send them to search out the land. Their mission was not to determine whether or not they should take the land. God had already determined that. It was to report on what the land was like. Was it heavily populated? Was it fertile and fruitful? Were there walled cities? Were they heavily fortified?

After forty days and nights, the spies returned with a divided report. There were two who said, "Go" and ten who said, "No." They all agreed, "Surely it is a land that flows with milk and honey. It is everything God said it was. 'Nevertheless . . .' nevertheless, there are giants in the land and there are walled cities that are heavily fortified and we were in their sight and our own sight as grasshoppers" (Numbers 13:26–33, KJV).

If you ever see yourself as a grasshopper, you will begin to act like a grasshopper, and that's how the Israelites saw themselves. In those moments the giants looked bigger than God. Their fears were greater than their faith and their obstacles outweighed their opportunities.

Fear soon spread throughout the camp and the people began to accuse Moses of bringing them to the wilderness to die. The "Back to Egypt Committee" called an emergency meeting and voted to go back to Egypt. They preferred the security of slavery to the risk of freedom (Num. 14:1–4).

Joshua and Caleb were the only two believing (faith-filled) spies. They encouraged the people to trust God and go forward in faith. Caleb spoke up, "If the LORD is pleased with us, he will lead us into that land, a land flowing with milk and honey, and will give it to us" (Num 14:8). In other words, "Taking the land will be a piece of cake."

But the people refused to believe. So the Lord said, ". . . not one of them will ever see the land I promised on oath to their forefathers. No one who has treated me with contempt will ever see it. But because my servant Caleb has a different spirit and follows me wholeheartedly, I will bring him into the land he went to . . ." (Num. 14:23–24).

Because of their unbelief they would be forced to wander in the wilderness of the Sinai Peninsula for the next forty years—one year for each day the spies had searched out the land.

The Israelites' journey was marked more by tombstones than milestones, as one-by-one every man and woman above twenty-years-of-age died and were buried in the wilderness. They would not be allowed to enter the Promised Land because of their lack of faith.

While these were years of suffering and hardship, and of discipline and death, they were also years of miracles as the Lord showed his power and faithfulness to them. He could be trusted to meet their every need.

God led them with a pillar of cloud by day and fire by night to assure them of his presence. He made water to flow from rocks to quench their thirst. He sent manna from heaven for their daily bread. And when they encountered enemies, the Lord gave them victory. The Scripture tells of God's complete care for the Israelites, "For forty years you sustained them in the desert; they lacked nothing, their clothes did not wear out nor did their feet become swollen" (Nehemiah 9:21).

After the years of wandering, God's people were brought to the border of the Promised Land again. The giants were still there, but this time there was no hesitancy. They knew if they wanted milk and honey on their bread they had to go where the giants were. Caleb, who survived the wilderness wandering because of his faith, even asked for the mountainous region of Horeb where the giants lived. To our knowledge he encountered only three of them. The giants were, as they most always are, mostly in their minds. And the land was soon conquered.

We all have to go through wilderness experiences from time to time—times of trial and testing, death and disappointment. They can take lots of shapes. They may be a sickness or an accident. They may be a wayward child or a disappointing marriage. They may be a financial reversal or even the death of a loved one. In those times, the Lord can be trusted to get us through the wilderness, if we trust him. As God led Israel through the wilderness he gave them leadership, food, and protection. He will also care for us. And when we face giants, he will give us victory.

There are times for the modern church, much like the church in the wilderness, when the obstacles seem to outweigh the opportunities. Times when the giants look bigger than God and the fears of some are greater than their faith. In those days, those of us in the older generation ought to be cheerleaders for progress. We ought to stand like Caleb and Joshua and say, "Come on church, with God's help we can do what is set before us." Listen, "I was young and now I am old, yet I have never seen the righteous forsaken or their children begging bread." The Lord is faithful.

▬ Cut the Electronics Off and Be Quiet ▬

Second, Eli teaches us that God is faithful to reveal his will for our life, if we will listen to his voice.

Eli was the aged priest who worked in the tabernacle after Israel had settled in the Promised Land. Samuel's mother had dedicated her young son to the Lord's service and so Samuel, at twelve-years-of-age, served Eli as an altar boy in the tabernacle.

One night while Samuel was in bed, he heard a voice calling him. He assumed it was the voice of Eli so he went to the room of the aged priest and asked if he had called. Eli had not called and told Samuel he had not. He told him to go on back to bed and go to sleep.

Samuel went back to his room and he heard the voice a second time. Once again he assumed it was the voice of Eli, so he went back to Eli's room to ask if he had called. Again Eli said that he had not, and told Samuel to go back to bed. Samuel heard the voice calling a third time and once again went to Eli to ask if he had called.

Eli had heard the voice of God before. He knew what it was like for God to speak to a person. So he said to young Samuel, go back to your room and if you hear the voice again, say "Speak, LORD, for your servant is listening" (1 Samuel 3:9).

Samuel went back to his room and once again the Lord spoke to him. This time he responded as Eli told him, "Speak, LORD, for your servant is listening." The Lord then said, "See, I am about to do something in Israel that will make the ears of everyone who hears of it tingle" [ring] (1 Sam. 3:10–11). And with that Samuel became the spiritual and political leader of Israel who unified the tribes and brought about a national revival.

Someone has said, "The two greatest days in a person's life are the day he is born and the day he discovers why he was born." But how do we know why we were born? The Lord reveals it to us. The manufacturer always knows why he made a product. But to know God's plan, the reason why you were born (and there is a reason), you have to listen to his voice. God speaks today just like he has in other generations. The problem is *we aren't listening.*

There are so many voices speaking to us today that God has a hard time getting through. Young people especially, are constantly listening to other voices, with their iPods, cell phones, and radios blaring; they can't hear the voice of God.

If you want to hear God's voice, you've got to be quiet. You need to shut out all the noise and listen. God doesn't shout, he whispers. And if you aren't listening, you can miss the voice of God all together. Jesus said, "Let the man who has ears to hear, hear." The fact that you've got ears to hear doesn't mean you are hearing. If you've got ears, listen! The Scriptures say, ". . . Today, if you hear his voice, do not harden your hearts . . ." (Hebrews 3:7–8).

I know God speaks because he called me. You say, "Did you hear an audible voice?" No, he spoke much louder than that. He spoke to my spirit.

But sometimes it takes an old man like Eli to help a young man like Samuel recognize the voice of God. We all may need that occasionally. R.E.B. Baylor, after whom Baylor University was named, was both a lawyer and a preacher in early Texas history. As a respected jurist, he was a district judge and later served on the Supreme Court of the Republic of Texas. He taught the first law courses at Baylor University when it was located in Independence, Texas.

Often when Baylor went to a city he would hold court in the daytime and preach a revival meeting at night. That way he got them coming and going. After one revival service he called on a fellow lawyer, Richard Ellis, to close the service in prayer. Bro. Ellis prayed with such pathos that when he was through Baylor sought him out, put his arm around his shoulder and said to him, "Bro. Ellis oughten you to be preaching the gospel?" Richard Ellis responded, "I left Virginia to get away from preaching the gospel." And Baylor said to him, "Richard, you've been running long enough."[3]

In those days the church often walked in such close fellowship with God that they often knew when God was speaking to a person before the person did. At times the person wasn't listening and the church was. How many times has it happened in our lives that somebody else knew God's will for our life before we knew it? Thank God for churches like that.

When I surrendered to the ministry years ago, several members came up to me and said, "We knew this was going to happen. We knew God was calling you to preach." They were so in tune with the will of God that they knew his will before I did.

We must be listening to God's voice and we must help others to listen also. How long has it been since we prayed with such intensity and persistency that God touched our heart and said there is a young person that I am speaking to? And then we cultivated them and encouraged them in God's service?

That's a part of the work of the church, and we have largely neglected it today.

It may very well be that the vitality of the church should be measured not by how many it has in Sunday School or how big its buildings or budget is, but by how many from the congregation are answering the call of God to Christian service.

Sometimes it takes an old man to teach a young man how to recognize the voice of God.

Listen, "I was young and now I am old, yet I have never seen the righteous forsaken or their children begging bread." God's promises are unfailing. His mercy and grace endures forever. He does speak if we'll just listen. He calls if we'll be attentive.

You may say, "Yes, but I'm an older person. Does God have anything for me? Abraham was seventy-five when God called him and God would use Abraham to bless the world. Moses was eighty when God sent him to deliver Israel from Egyptian bondage.

Anna was eighty-four and still serving in the temple. John was ninety when he wrote Revelation. I was sixty-eight when I became Dean of Truett Seminary. God will be faithful no matter what our age is. The question is; will we be faithful?

▬ The Dark Night of the Soul ▬

Third, David teaches us that God is faithful to get us home safely at the end of life, if we will follow the shepherd.

I'm not sure how old David was when he wrote the 23rd Psalm. Caleb was eighty-five when he went into the

Promised Land. Eli was ninety when he was serving in the tabernacle. I know this about David, he was not in the springtime of youth, nor the vitality of summer, he was in the winter of old age when he said one day:

> The Lord is my shepherd, I shall not be in want. He makes me lie down in green pastures, he leads me beside quiet waters, he restores my soul. He guides me in paths of righteousness for his name's sake. Even though I walk through the valley of the shadow of death, I will fear no evil, for you are with me; your rod and your staff, they comfort me. You prepare a table before me in the presence of my enemies. You anoint my head with oil; my cup overflows. Surely goodness and love will follow me all the days of my life, and I will dwell in the house of the Lord forever.
>
> Psalm 23:1–6

The Lord is paying us no compliment when he compares us to sheep. Sheep are among the most helpless and defenseless creatures there are. They can't see more than ten to fifteen feet in front of them. They don't have horns, claws, or fangs to defend themselves. They can't run very fast. And they aren't very smart. Have you ever seen one in a circus? Sheep need a shepherd.

David begins simply, "The Lord is 'my' shepherd." Don't miss that personal pronoun "my." Everything takes on new meaning when you put the word *my* in front of it. It is one thing to say "there's a house." It's something else to say "there is *my house*." It is one thing to say "that's a girl." It's something else to say "that's *my girl*." It is one thing to say "that's a baby." It's something else to say "that's *my baby*." Our relationship with the Lord takes on new meaning when we can say "The Lord is *my shepherd*."

David then says, "He makes me lie down in green pastures, he leads me beside quiet waters, he restores my soul. He guides me in paths of righteousness for his name's sake."

A few months ago I visited an eighty-seven-year-old lady, Margieree Eaton. She often listened to our services on television and wanted to meet me. So, one day I made my way to Athens, a little town thirty-five miles from Tyler and found her rundown mobile home out on a country road.

She came to the door in a wheelchair. I went inside and we had a wonderful visit about God's mercy and grace. When I got ready to leave, she sort of summed it all up with these words, "Pastor, the Lord sustains me." That's what David is saying here. "The Lord sustains me."

But life is not all green pastures and still waters. Sometimes the green pastures become rough and rocky hills, and the still waters become stormy and turbulent seas. When life tumbles in, what then? When we face what F. Scott Fitzgerald called "the dark night of the soul,"[4] what then? David says, "Even though I walk through the valley of the shadow of death, I will fear no evil, for you are with me; your rod and your staff, they comfort me." The Lord is with us through the dark experiences of life.

But that's not the last word for us. He adds, "You prepare a table before me in the presence of my enemies. You anoint my head with oil; my cup overflows. Surely goodness and love will follow me all the days of my life, and I will dwell in the house of the LORD forever."

It was a thousand years later that Jesus came saying, "I am the good shepherd. The good shepherd lays down his life for the sheep" (John 10:11). On the cross of Calvary Jesus gave his life for us. This guarantees those of us who trust him a safe trip home.

Life is a journey to eternity, and at the end of the road is God. God is faithful to keep his people. When we get to the end, God will be there to see us across the river.

Listen, "I was young and now I am old, yet I have never seen the righteous forsaken or their children begging bread." If age teaches us anything, it teaches us not to let fear hold us back. Like Caleb, if we want milk and honey on our bread, we must go where the giants are. Like Eli taught Samuel, if we want to know God's plan for our lives, we must be quiet and listen to his voice.

And like David, if we want to arrive home safely at the end of life, we must follow the shepherd.

Tony Blair, who served as the Prime Minister of England, is a Christian. He said when he was ten-years-old his father suffered a severe stroke and was rushed to the hospital. The doctors were uncertain of his survival. His mother, who tried to keep some sense of normality in her children's lives, sent them on to school that morning.

The headmaster (who was ordained), in an attempt to provide comfort, suggested that they kneel together and pray for his father's recovery.

Tony said, "I whispered to my friend, 'I'm afraid my father doesn't believe in God.'"

The teacher replied, "That doesn't matter, God believes in him."[5]

I hope you'll remember, God believes in you.

He believes in you so much he gave his son to die for your sins and salvation.

His love is everlasting.

He is faithful to his word.

He will see you home safely.

--- N O T E S ---

1. Ronald W. Reagan, *An American Life: Ronald Reagan, The Autobiography* (New York, NY: Pocket Books, 1990), 179.

2. http://www.presidency.ucsb.edu/ws/?pid=35897. Accessed 5/23/2014.

3. Letter from R.E.B. Baylor to James Stribling, cited in Robert A. Baker, *The Blooming Desert* (Waco: Word Books, 1970), 70.

4. F. Scott Fitzgerald, *The Crack-Up* (New York: New Directions Books, 1945, 1993), 75.

5. http://amyfound.org/writing_resources/amy_internet_syndicate/articles/rusty_wright/rw78.html. Accessed 5/23/2014.

9

Making an Impact for God

But when they did not find them, they dragged Jason and some other brothers before the city officials, shouting: "These men (Paul and Silas) who have caused trouble all over the world have now come here . . ."

Acts 17:6

The local church has been a large part of my walk with God. It was in a church that I first heard the gospel. It was in the church that I first responded to Christ. It was in the church that I was baptized. It was in the church that I first felt and answered the call to preach. It was in the church that I was ordained. It was in the church that I was married. It is from the church I'll be buried. And it has been the church that I have served for over sixty years.

But the church is not what it was in those early days. Of course, neither am I. It has changed, and so have I. In those earlier years, the church not only had a huge impact on me, it had an impact on all of society. But through the years the influence and impact of the church has waned significantly.

The early church leaders were described as "those who have turned the world upside down."

Wherever those early missionaries went they either created a riot or a revival. The people of God ought to create one or the other in our day. The worst thing that can happen to a preacher or a church is for either of them to be in a given place for a reasonable period of time, and no one knows or cares that they have been there. I have always said, "I would rather be cussed than not discussed at all."

Those of us who serve in and through the church, whether we are lay people or ministers; can lead our church to make a difference—to have an impact.

How do we do that? What are the marks of a high-impact church?

> It is a church on fire.
> It is a church in harmony.
> It is a church at work.
> It is a church on its knees.
> It is a church in the streets.

━ In Simplicity and Power ━

First, a high-impact church is a church on fire.

Fire is often associated with the word of God: God spoke to Moses out of a burning bush (Exodus 3:2); when God gave the Ten Commandments there was fire on the mountain (Exodus 24:17); when Jeremiah resolved he would not speak the word of God again, ". . . his word is in my heart like a fire, a fire shut up in my bones. I am weary of holding it in . . ." (Jeremiah 20:9); and when the Holy Spirit came upon the disciples on the day of Pentecost, they saw what seemed to be "tongues of fire" (Acts 2:3).

Whatever a church may do or leave undone, it must have a pulpit on fire with the word of God. That fire may start in a number of places: in the prayer closet, among the deacons, in the women's missionary group; but it must soon spread to the pulpit if it is to be a high-impact church.

Whenever and wherever the word of God is preached in simplicity and in power things begin to happen. E.F. "Preacher" Hallock was pastor of the First Baptist Church of Norman, Oklahoma for forty years. In those years he touched the lives of thousands of students who passed through the University of Oklahoma. He began as a Methodist minister in Kansas. His church conducted a revival meeting. During that meeting he fell under conviction, went to the front of the church, and confessed he had never been saved.

As he began to study the Bible, he realized he had never been baptized correctly, i.e., by immersion. So he got immersed and decided to become a Baptist and start over.

He said late in life, "I went to be a pastor of a small church and while there I determined I was going to master the word of God. But err I realized it the word had mastered me."

That's the way it is: "For the word of God is living and active. Sharper than any double-edged sword, it penetrates even to dividing soul and spirit, joints and marrow; it judges the thoughts and attitudes of the heart" (Hebrews 4:12).

It even has the power to change the preacher's life. Elias Keach formed the second Pennsylvania Baptist Church in 1688. The church, located in Pennepek, began with twelve members and Keach served as their pastor.

Elias Keach, the son of English Baptist pastor Benjamin Keach, had arrived in America in 1687. Elias Keach was not a professing Christian but rather a wild young man. Because he was the son of a minister and dressed like a minister, Keach was soon invited to preach at a Baptist gathering.

He accepted this invitation, confident that he could deliver a sermon that would equal one preached by his father.

While he was in the midst of his sermon, "the enormity of his sin dawned upon him. He was overcome by remorse [and] confessed his imposture." His audience, most likely shaken by this extreme show of emotion, soon discovered that the preacher had been "soundly converted—under his own preaching!"[1]

**That is high-impact preaching.
That's making a difference.**

E-Harmony.com

Second, a high-impact church is a church in harmony.

Ever hear an orchestra warming up? Everyone is doing his own thing. Then the conductor comes in and the audience applauds. He hasn't done a thing yet. He taps on the rostrum with his baton and the musicians all begin to play in harmony. The Holy Spirit is the conductor, and he creates harmony in the church when he is in control.

Baptists have always had a difficult time living together in harmony. Even the first Baptist church formed in history ended up in a split. A group of Christians in England became convinced that the Church of England was corrupt and in error, and sought to separate from it. John Smyth and Thomas Helwys, after studying the Bible, particularly the New Testament, concluded that a true church would be made up of believers who publicly confess Christ as Lord and who experience believers' baptism. Consequently, they concluded that the Church of England was not the true church, and they attempted to worship according to the dictates of their own conscience.

But there was no religious liberty in England at the time. So they went to Holland, the only place in Europe where religious liberty existed. In 1609 they formed the first Baptist church in history. Because none of the people had been baptized as believers, Smyth baptized himself. He probably poured water over himself (baptism by immersion would not come for another thirty years) and then baptized the others; thereby forming a new church.

Later, Smyth came into contact with a Mennonite congregation in Amsterdam and determined that this group comprised a true church, and he concluded he should have sought baptism from one of their ministers. He began to question the validity of his self-baptism.

Controversy arose in the new church concerning the succession of Christian ministry from the apostolic times. Most members agreed with Smyth that only the ministers who had been properly baptized could administer baptism. Helwys and ten or twelve others disagreed. As a result, the church split into two groups over the issue, and in 1610 a minority led by Helwys excommunicated Smyth and thirty-one others.[2] That's the way we Baptists are.

How do you keep harmony in a church? The Scriptures speak to this subject often. The Apostle Paul writes, "Live in harmony with one another. Do not be proud, but be willing to associate with people of low position. Do not be conceited" (Romans 12:16).

Freely translated, he is telling us we should look at things from the other person's point of view. We should not put ourselves above others, but rather, humble ourselves. We shouldn't act like "know-it-alls" and we should work at getting along.

Then later in this passage Paul says, "If it is possible, as far as it depends on you, live at peace with everyone" (Rom. 12:18).

To my knowledge, I have only had one man in fifty years of ministry I could not live with peaceably. I tried and tried, but there was just no way.

After I accepted the call to the Green Acres Baptist Church in Tyler, and before I left San Marcos, I received a call one day from an anonymous caller. He asked, "Are you going to Tyler?" I replied, "Yes." He then replied, "Watch out for so and so. He is a vampire. He will eat your guts out."

I asked, "Who is this?" And there was a click on the other end of the line as he hung up.

You don't quickly forget a call like that, so I tucked the information away in the corner of my mind. Sure enough, shortly after coming to Tyler I was in conflict with this man. He was a deacon but he never attended meetings unless there was controversy. Then he wanted to come and tell the group what to do.

He was also well-known as a social drinker. Traditionally deacons have been total abstainers from the use of alcohol, and he violated that principle. This troubled a number of our men so they appointed a committee to develop a set of policies for our deacons. The committee took its recommendation to the deacon body and they approved it. They took it to the church and the church approved it. Then a letter was sent to all of our deacons informing them of the policy.

By return mail, I received a threatening letter from this man saying that he had known of churches that had split over less than this. So I picked up the phone, called him, and made an appointment to visit with him.

In our visit he accused me of throwing him out of the deacon body. I responded, "No, no, I am not throwing you out of anything." Then I recounted the whole process and said, "These are the policies, and if you want to abide by them you are welcome to be part of the group. Otherwise you are excluding yourself. I am not excluding you."

We parted without the issue being resolved. Thereafter for the next sixteen years every time he was in the hospital or every time there was a crisis in his life, I visited him and ministered to his family, but every time he brought this matter up.

One day in the sixteenth year of my pastorate, he visited me in my study. By this time he was an old man walking with a cane. He sat down and began to rehash this issue. I just reached over in my file drawer and pulled out the threatening letter he had written me years before. I had saved it because of the phone call I mentioned earlier. I slid it across the desk and asked him, "Whose signature is on that letter?" He replied, "It is mine."

I asked, "What is the date on that letter?" He looked at it and said, "February 1973." I said to him, "Friend, that was sixteen years ago. You need to let go of this. You have a problem. I don't have a problem. I don't know what you are going to do about your problem."

With that he jumped up and stormed out of my office as fast as a man with a walking cane can storm. Shortly after that I moved to Dallas to become president of the Annuity Board (now Guidestone Financial Resources). Every time I wrote a new book I sent him a complimentary copy with a nice note written in the flyleaf. I was doing what the Scripture says. I was heaping "burning coals on his head" (Romans 12:20). I figured where he was going, he needed to get used to the heat.

But when his wife died, he asked me to do her funeral. After the funeral I visited him and he once again brought up this subject. I left without it being resolved. When he died his two sons asked me to conduct his funeral. I couldn't do it because I was in a revival meeting that week, but I would have loved to. There are some funerals you don't want to miss.

The Scriptures are right, "If it is possible, as far as it depends on you, live at peace with everyone." But sometimes it is not possible because they won't let you.

▬ Hands and Feet Amputated ▬

Third, a high-impact church is a church at work. The Apostle Paul often in Scripture speaks of the church as the body of Christ. As our body has many parts and yet is one, so the church, the body of Christ has many members. To these members he gives gifts, i.e., special abilities and endowments, to equip us to do the work of God.

Paul mentions these gifts in five places in the Scriptures. The lists are never exhaustive, but illustrative. In Romans 12 he lists seven gifts of the Spirit. They are: prophecy-preaching; ministry-helping others; teaching; exhorting-encouragement; giving; ruling-administration or leading; and mercy-working with the downtrodden.

Paul suggests that if you have the gift of preaching that your sermons be strong and helpful. If you have the gift of ministry, don't try to take over, but help people according to their needs. If you have the gift of teaching, stick to God's word and teach it well.

If you have the gift of exhorting or encouragement then be careful not to be bossy. If you have the gift of giving, keep your eye out for people in need and respond quickly to them without fanfare. If you have the gift of administration and are put in charge of things, then make something happen. And if you have the gift of mercy, (working with the downtrodden) don't get depressed. Keep a smile on your face.

Every believer has been given some gift in order to do the work of God, and we need to discover and use those gifts in the service of God.

Rick Warren reminds us, "The New Testament church is the body of Christ but for the last one-hundred years the hands and feet have been amputated and the church has just been a mouth and mostly it has been known for what it is against."[3]

The challenge is to discover and put to use the gift(s) God has given to us.

The late Bum Phillips, coach of the Houston Oilers and the New Orleans Saints professional football teams, was a master of one-liners. Like most coaches he worked day and night. While coaching the Oilers, his wife called him and said, "Bum, I believe you love football more than you love me." Bum replied, "Yes, but I love you more than I love basketball."

After his retirement, a reporter asked him what he did with his time. He replied, "I don't do anything and I don't start that until noon."

His star running back while with the Houston Oilers was Earl Campbell, the Heisman Trophy winner from the University of Texas and an all-pro player. Bum was asked once by a reporter, "Is Earl Campbell in a class all by himself?" Bum replied, "Earl may not be in a class by himself, but whatever class he's in, it doesn't take long to call the roll."

One of his best lines was when the Oilers were considering drafting Earl Campbell. One of his scouts said to Bum, "Earl Campbell is a sprinter, you know. He is not a distance runner. He can't run a mile. Do you still want to draft him?"

Bum responded, "Sure, I just won't give him the ball when it is third down and a mile."

A good coach knows the gifts and abilities of his players and uses them to the advantage of the team. Some can block and tackle. Some can run. Some can pass. Some can catch passes. A coach knows what his players can do. The pastor is a player-coach who knows his team and helps to develop their gifts to be used for the maximum in God's service. A high-impact church is a church that utilizes everybody in the work of God.

The "Three Open" Prayer

Fourth, a high-impact church is a church on its knees.

The Scriptures remind us, "The prayer of a righteous man is powerful and effective" (James 5:16).

E. Stanley Jones used to say, "I am better or worse as I pray more or less." We all are, and the church is. We need to pray about everything, especially about winning the lost.

Warren Wiersby talks about a "three open" prayer. "Lord open his door to me. Open his heart to you. Open my mouth to say the right thing."

A church praying like that on its knees, will soon be a high-impact church.

He Done It

Fifth, a high-impact church is a church in the streets.

In the beginning days of his ministry, Billy Graham's crusades were like most of society: segregated. But two years before there was forced integration in the public schools, he decided he would no longer have segregated meetings.

It was in Jackson, Mississippi, of all places, when he determined this. It was the custom in those days to put up ropes to separate the blacks from the whites. When Billy asked for the ropes to be taken down, the ushers refused. So, Billy took them down himself and began integrating the meetings. After that, he would not hold revival meetings in a place unless the crowd could be integrated.

He became friends with Martin Luther King, Jr. and sought his advice on racial issues. They met in privacy and each supported the ministry of the other. Martin Luther King said to Billy Graham, "You stay in the stadiums and hold integrated crusades and I'll stay in the streets. I may get killed there, but you will be doing more good in the stadiums than I could do."

There are some things that can be done in the stadium, and there are some things that can only be done in the streets. If we are going to have high-impact churches we must do more than meet in the stadiums. We must take to the streets.

This may be our greatest weakness today. The first church in Texas was formed by Daniel Parker. Mexican law forbade any church being "formed" in Texas except a Roman Catholic one, so he "formed" a church in Illinois and moved it to Texas in 1834. It was an "anti-church," "anti-missionary," "anti-Sunday School," "anti-education," "anti-everything" environment.

In time, Parker formed several other churches and they grouped together in what were called "do nothing" associations. The association met, recorded the fact they had met, set the time and place of their next meeting, and adjourned.[4]

That sounds like a lot of churches I know. They meet, record the fact that they met, set a time and place for the next meeting, and adjourn. Will Rogers said of the presidency of Calvin Coolidge, "The country wanted nothing done, and he done it."[5]

It is amazing what men will do to forward their own cause. Pat Neff was once governor of Texas and president of Baylor University. When he was running for governor he wrote a letter to everyone in the state named Neff. He said, "You don't know me but the fact that your name is Neff is reason enough to support me."

The only other instance of a candidate writing individuals with the same surname would occur a half a century later by then Texas Lieutenant Governor Preston Smith. Journalist and author Jimmy Banks has written that when Smith was running for governor, he realized there had never been a Texas governor named Smith. He sent letters to 47,000 "Smiths" in Texas asking, "Don't you think it is about time one of us was governor?"[6]

The church today needs to go on that kind of offensive. If men will do that to be elected to public office, what should we do to bring people into the kingdom of God?

Some unknown poet put it this way:

They will not come, they must be brought.
They will not seek, they must be sought.
They will not learn, they must be taught.

That is our mission and challenge.

**We must be equal to it if we are going
to be high-impact churches.**

──────────── N O T E S ────────────

1. Pamela R. Durso and Keith E. Durso, *The Story of Baptists in the United States* (Brentwood, TN: Baptist History and Heritage Society, 2006), 36.

2. Keith E. Durso, *No Armor for the Back* (Macon, GA: Mercer University Press, 2007), 18–19.

3. http://usatoday30.usatoday.com/news/opinion/editorials/2006-06-04-on-religion_x.htm. Accessed 5/23/2014.

4. Harry Leon McBeth, *Texas Baptists: A Sesquicentennial History* (Dallas, Texas: BaptistWay Press, 1998), 22–23.

5. Shannon, Rober C. "Let Me Illustrate." *The Pulpit Digest* March/April 1984: 118. Print.

6. Dorothy Blodgett, Terrell Blodgett, and David L. Scott, *The Life of Pat Neff* (Austin, TX: Homeplace Publishers, 2007), 71.

10

Growing Old with God

Even to your old age and gray hairs I am he, I am he who will sustain you. I have made you and I will carry you; I will sustain you and I will rescue you.

Isaiah 46:4

Billy Graham said, "I had been taught all of my life how to die, but no one had ever taught me how to grow old."[1]

We'd better learn, because old age inevitably comes to all of us if we live long enough. In fact, growing old is one of the things you can do without any effort. Every day 10,000 people turn sixty-five, the generally accepted retirement age. Of course there's nothing sacred about sixty-five as the age to retire.

In 1889, German Chancellor Bismark pioneered old age pension plans and sixty-five was arbitrarily selected as a pensioners' age. Nearly twenty years later, England adopted a pension plan that set the age at seventy, and later dropped it back to sixty-five. In Sweden it was set at fifty-seven then changed to sixty-five. And, finally, the designers of the United States Social Security Act of 1935 picked sixty-five. This age was set by consensus, not for any scientific or genetic reason.

People are also living longer. There are over 90,000 people in the United States 100-years-of-age or older. When that happens, people retiring at age sixty-five still have one-third of their life ahead of them.

I was attending a conference in Arkansas several years ago and met a 101-year-old pastor who had preached a sermon on his 100th birthday. I asked him, "How do you get to be 100?" He replied, "It's easy. You just get to be 99 and then be ver-r-ry careful." We are living longer, but are we living better? We are adding years to our life, but are we adding life to our years? We need to know how to live life to the full. We need to know how to make the most of our retirement years.

I offer five suggestions:

>) Take care of your assets.
>) Stay as active as you can as long as you can.
>) Stay close to your friends.
>) Don't retire from life.
>) Finish well.

▬ Know What's Important ▬

First, take care of your assets.

A person's assets are the entire property of that person. But God's value system is entirely different. Look at what the Bible teaches:

>) It is better to get wisdom than to get silver and gold (Proverbs 16:16).
>) A good name is rather to be chosen than great riches (Proverbs 22:1).
>) Who can find a virtuous woman for her price is far above rubies (Proverbs 31:10).

Good judgment, a good name, and a good spouse; those are the real assets of life. All three must be guarded.

Keep your mind active as long as possible. It is tragic when our body outlives our mind. Reading, table games and good conversation will help.

And your good name is invaluable. A good name can take a lifetime to build and can be ruined in an instant by one single compromise or indiscretion.

But your spouse will be by far your greatest asset. If she/he is your greatest asset then she/he deserves at least as much attention and care as your investment portfolio. I have made lots of deals in my life. I have bought stocks and bonds, houses and land, oil and gas interests; but the best deal I ever made was when I got Cathy to be my wife.

We celebrated our 60th wedding anniversary September 2, 2013. I asked Cathy a few weeks before, "Where would you like me to take you for our anniversary?" She replied, "Take me to some place I haven't been in a long time." I said, "How about the kitchen?" Did I mention that my sweet wife has a wonderful sense of humor?

A couple of years ago I asked her on the morning of our anniversary, "Honey, did you ever in your wildest dreams think you would be married to me for fifty-eight years?" She replied, "Paul, you were never part of my wildest dreams."

Actually it is a miracle that we are still together. We were so different. She was a city girl and accustomed to city ways. I was a country boy. My family came to the city when I was in the third grade but we kept our country ways. One of the things that used to characterize country ladies, like my mother, was that they made homemade biscuits with every meal. That was the only bread available in the country. And my mother was a master of it.

She had a wooden bowl and would put in some flour, a pinch of baking soda, some baking powder, a dash of salt, and shortening. Then she would knead it for a few minutes and it was ready to bake. She never measured anything. She had done it so many times that she could do it in her sleep. She then broke up the dough and put it in a pan and in the oven. In a few minutes out came some of the most delicious biscuits you've ever tasted.

Cathy ate at our house a few times before we got married. After we got married she decided she was going to bake me some biscuits. I wouldn't want to be critical of them, but when she took them out of the oven they looked like Ritz Crackers that were anorexic. I made a great mistake. I said to her, "Why can't you cook biscuits like my mother?" She replied, "When you make dough like my daddy, I'll make bread like your momma." And I learned a great lesson that day on effective communication within a marriage.

The fact is, no matter how old we are or how long we have been married, we need to keep working at making our marriage a success.

A few years ago I was called on to do a wedding ceremony for a couple on the 69th anniversary of their first date together. Winn and Sue had been sweethearts in Tyler but they went away to college and they met and married other people.

Winfred went to Texas Tech and Sue went to Mary Hardin Baylor. Sue had been a widow for thirty years and Winfred a widower for five years when they came back to Tyler, got reacquainted, and decided to get married. They asked me to perform the ceremony.

I was happy to be a part of this special occasion and walked out on the platform. Sue made it up to the altar fairly well by herself. She was eighty-seven years old. Winn had a little more trouble. He was ninety and on a walker. His seventy-year-old son had to help him up there.

I began the ceremony, "Winn, do you take Sue to be your lawfully wedded wife, do you promise before God and these witnesses to love her, comfort her, honor her, to keep her in sickness and in health, and forsaking all others to keep thee only unto her so long as you both shall live. Do you so promise?"

Instead of saying "I do," he said, "I'll try." I like that. Ninety-years-old and still trying.

That's what we all have to do, as long as we live. And if we do, our love will flourish and will return rich dividends. Historian Will Durant, who enjoyed a wonderful marriage said, "The love we have in our youth is superficial compared to the love that an old man has for his wife." Amen!

▬ Stay Out of the Rocking Chair ▬

Second, stay active for as long as you can.

I was in Japan years ago speaking at a missions meeting and learned that one of the missionaries was getting ready to retire in a few weeks. Someone asked him what he intended to do in retirement. He said, "The first six months I intend to sit in a rocking chair. After that, I may rock." Too many people think of retirement as sitting in a rocking chair and doing nothing.

A lady asked her husband, "What are you going to do today?" He replied, "Nothing." She said, "That's what you did yesterday." He said, "Yep, I didn't finish."

But I remind you that life is like water skiing, you slow down . . . and you go down. So in retirement get up and get moving. Any doctor will tell you moderate exercise will produce dramatic benefits for your health. It will help keep you out of the doctor's office. And there'll be enough of that anyway.

I have a friend who went to the doctor. The doctor gave him six months to live. He didn't pay his bill so the doctor gave him another six months. The doctor said to Mrs. Brown, "Mrs. Brown, your check came back." She said, "Yes, so did my arthritis."

Comedian Bill Cosby refers to physical fitness as "temple keeping." Our bodies are the temple of the Holy Spirit. And then with humor he says, "I have watched my body change from a 'temple' into a 'storefront church.'"

So don't sit around collecting dust.
Keep moving as long as you can.

▰ A Vanished Friend ▰

Third, stay close to your friends.

Elizabeth Barrett Browing, the poet, once asked Charles Kingsly, the novelist, the secret to his beautiful life. He thought for a moment and then he replied, "I have a friend."

All of us have been enriched by our friendships. But I've learned through the years that friends are not forever. In the last five years I've conducted the funeral of 129 of my friends. I buried my CPA, one of my bankers, my funeral director, my grocer, my clothier, my brother-in-law, my sister, my niece, and 121 others.

I have buried everything but a lawyer. Do lawyers ever die?

I don't tell lawyer jokes. It's dangerous. But I did hear Congressman Ralph Hall recently tell about a young man who had just graduated from law school and was feeling his importance.

The young lawyer was to catch a plane at DFW airport and arrived late. The plane was just getting ready to pull away from the terminal when he rushed down the concourse and banged on the door and said to the stewardess inside, "I've got a ticket for this flight and I need to be on it. Let me in." You know of course that once the stewardess closes that door she won't open it for anybody. But he kept banging and said, "Look, I'm a lawyer and I will sue you personally and I'll sue the airline if you don't let me in."

The stewardess turned to a man in first class and said to him, "Lawyers are jerks!" The man responded, "I resent that."

She said, "Oh sir, I'm sorry, I didn't realize you were a lawyer." He replied, "I'm not, I'm a jerk."

This past year I buried an unusual friend. She named me as the executor of her estate and stated that she wanted me to conduct her funeral service. After that, I was to accompany her body to Decatur, Texas for burial. I was to remain at the grave until it was covered and the flowers were put on it. She even specified I was to be paid $500. I must have been thinking of that $500 rather than how far Decatur was from Tyler and how long all of this would take when I agreed to all her demands.

Decatur is three-and-a-half hours from Tyler; then it's another three-and-a-half-hours back. Then there's the time spent waiting for the grave to be covered, and the time to eat lunch, and before you know it a good ten-hour-day is gone.

We had the service one day and made the trip to Decatur two days later. As we were preparing to leave Tyler, I told the funeral directors, "I want you to call ahead and tell the cemetery workers to have a front end loader at that grave and running when we arrive. And, when I say 'amen,' the first sound I want to hear is not a sob from the family, but the thud of dirt hitting that casket. I don't want to stand around all day while that grave is covered."

Then I said, "Just in case . . . just in case, I want you to put two shovels in the hearse because if that front end loader isn't there I've got 'shovel-ready jobs' for you two." They saw to it that the loader was there.

Our friends do slip away, so we need to enjoy them while we can. The poet put it this way:

Around The Corner

Around the corner I have a friend,
In this great city that has no end;
Yet the days go by and weeks rush on,
And before I know it, a year is gone,
And I see my old friend's face,
For life is a swift and terrible race.
He knows I like him just as well
As in the days when I rang his bell.
And he rang mine. We were younger then,
And now we are busy, tired men;
Tired with playing a foolish game,
Tired with trying to make a name.
"Tomorrow," I say, "I will call on Jim
Just to show that I'm thinking of him."
But tomorrow comes—and tomorrow goes,
And the distance between us grows and grows.
Around the corner!—yet miles away . . .
"Here's a telegram sir, *Jim died today*."
And that's what we get, and deserve in the end.
Around the corner, a vanished friend.[2]

Robert Louis Stevenson is credited with saying, "A friend is a gift you give yourself." And John Leonard reminds us, "It takes a long time to grow an old friend." Enjoy them while you can.

▬ Don't Fade Into the Sunset ▬

Fourth, don't retire from life.

When I retired from the Annuity Board at the age of sixty-four, I said to Bill Pinson, Executive Director of Texas Baptists at the time, "Bill, I'm going back to East Texas and fade into the sunset." But he said, "No, we can't let you do that. There's too much that needs to be done. I'll give you an assignment." He did and I set to work helping to strengthen the leadership in Texas Baptist churches.

I had a full preaching schedule for the next three years, so I stayed fairly busy. But at the age of sixty-seven Dr. Robert Sloan, president of Baylor University, asked me be the Dean of Truett Theological Seminary, a part of Baylor University.

It was unusual how that happened. At my recommendation and the recommendation of some others, another pastor was being considered for the job. The day he was to be interviewed I called Robert to see how the day went. He said, "Oh Paul, it's been a bad day. Howie turned me down." Then there was a long pause and he said to me, "Will you take it?"

Well, that's sort of like a couple standing at the altar and the bride deciding at the last minute she doesn't want to get married and the minister turns to the maid of honor and says, "Will you take him?" But I thought about it for a while and decided that's what I ought to do.

I agreed to go to Truett for three-and-a-half years and my tenure stretched into six-and-a-half years. It turned out that those were perhaps the most important six years of my life. In fact, I believe all I had ever done up until then was in preparation for that work. Little did I know that after I retired, I would do the most significant work of my life. I stayed there until I was seventy-four.

I came back to Tyler, and at age seventy-six, the First Baptist Church of Tyler was looking for an interim pastor and somebody gave them my name. They decided to work from resumes, and even though I had been their interim ten years earlier, and had lived a public life in Tyler for forty years; they wanted a resume from me. So when the staff member called to request mine she said to me, "They want your resume but I need to tell you that some people on the committee think you're too old."

So I sent them my resume with my high school picture attached.

I guess it worked because I got the job.

All of my life I've been told that Christians shouldn't retire, that there is nothing in the Bible about retirement, but I just recently learned otherwise. The Lord instructed Moses that at the age of fifty the Levites (assistants to the priests) should ". . . retire from their regular service and work no longer" (Numbers 8:25). No reason is given, but presumably it was because theirs was strenuous work and younger men could do it better.

So it's OK to retire from your job, but don't retire from life. There's too much left to do in life. In retirement you've got money to give, wisdom to share, skills to pass on, and experiences to draw from. It would be a terrible waste for you to not continue to invest in people and in God's kingdom.

What can retired people do?

You can be more active as a mentor to your grandchildren. Our grandchildren gave us a plaque last year that said, "Grandchildren are God's reward for not killing your own children."

You can pray. One of the most influential people in my life was my youth director when I was a teenager. I left for college and she went to another church. We wrote some, but it was close to fifty years before we chanced to meet again while serving on a committee. She was ninety at the time and she said, "Paul, I pray for you every day."

You can minister. When my mom was ninety-years-old she regularly visited the "old folks" in nursing homes. Mom was an uneducated country girl, but remarkable in many ways. She turned ninety-six one day and died the next. Her advancing age didn't prevent her from ministering to others.

You can work at the church. Dick Goad, a retired grocery executive, came to the church every Monday morning and duplicated and mailed about 250 tapes that had been ordered by our TV audience. It saved a church secretary a day's work.

You can write notes of encouragement. I wrote a friend recently who lost a son a few months ago. He replied, "Well . . . I had just about reached the end of my rope and your very nice note arrived. We never know what will give us a renewed breath of fresh air. You are very good to come up with the right words at the right time. Sue got some good news from the cancer clinic yesterday for which we are very grateful. Thank you for being my good friend."

You still have more to contribute.
So, retire from your job, but don't retire from life.

▬ Writing Your Legacy ▬

Finally, finish well.

The late Joe Paterno, long time coach at Penn State, was the winningest college football coach in history. He is a tragic example of someone who did not finish well. At eighty-five he had coached at Penn State for sixty-one years—forty-six as the head coach. His 409 victories were more than any other coach. He had five undefeated seasons, two national championships, and his teams played in thirty-one bowl games. His motto was, "Success with honor."

Joe's life was ruined not by what he did, but by what he failed to do. He failed to follow up on reports of improper behavior by one of the members of his staff. He failed to live by his own values.

The end result was that his statue at the university stadium was taken down, his name was removed from the university library that had been named in his honor, and he died in disgrace. It can happen. More than one runner has stumbled in the last lap of the race.

The Scriptures remind us, "Therefore, since we are surrounded by such a great cloud of witnesses, let us throw off everything that hinders and the sin that so easily entangles, and let us run with perseverance the race marked out for us. Let us fix our eyes on Jesus, the author and perfecter of our faith, who for the joy set before him endured the cross, scorning its shame, and sat down at the right hand of the throne of God" (Hebrews 12:1–2).

Keep your eyes on Jesus and finish well. The challenge of the risen Christ to us is, "Be faithful, even to the point of death, and I will give you the crown of life" (Revelation 2:10b). He didn't say be faithful until you're tired or until you're retired, but until you are *expired* . . . be faithful, *even to the point of death*.

That's the challenge we all face.

Vincent Van Gogh was one of the greatest painters of all time. Early in his life he wanted to be a pastor but he could not gain admittance to the seminary. So he became a volunteer missionary and worked in a poor mining district in Belgium. He was so dedicated and made so many sacrifices, that he intimidated the other missionaries and was fired from their missionary compound.

He turned to painting because he did not know what else to do. He died at the age of thirty-seven. The last five years of his life he painted 800 pictures, but sold only one. Just a couple of years ago an art dealer turned down twenty-five million dollars for one of his paintings.

Somewhere along the way Vincent Van Gogh said, "I wish not that my legacy be written on a building or in stone. I wish that my legacy be written on the heart of God."

Live with that goal in mind and you'll live life to the full.

Here is a promise you can bank on: "Even to your old age and gray hairs I am he, I am he who will sustain you. I have made you and I will carry you; I will sustain you and I will rescue you" (Isaiah 46:4).

God has been and will be faithful to us.

The question is; will we be faithful to him—to the end?

NOTES

1. Billy Graham, *Nearing Home: Life, Faith, and Finishing Well* (Nashville, Tennessee: Thomas Nelson, 2011), 93.

2. Charles Hanson Towne, "Around the Corner" from *A World of Windows and Other Poems* (New York: George H. Doran Company, 1919), 66.

11

Transitioning with God

You will all fall away, Jesus told them, for it is written: "I will strike the shepherd, and the sheep will be scattered."

Mark 14:27

If change is a part of life, so is transition. And times of transition are precarious for everyone—both for the individual and the church—especially a church that is experiencing a change in leadership..

For one thing, it can be a time of decline. When the leader leaves there are always other people who leave with him. They may have been thinking of changing churches for various reasons and this becomes a convenient time to make a move. By leaving now they are less likely to be missed by the church and there is no danger of meeting the pastor out in the community and having to explain their decision to him.

Others just drop out. They aren't mad or upset, like sheep they just wander off. This is doubly true if the pastor's leaving is a forced termination. Jesus alluded to this when he said: "I will strike the shepherd, and the sheep will be scattered" (Mark 14:27).

There are at least four groups in every church. There are those who like the staff person who was terminated no matter who he/she is. There are those who think the church should never fire anyone. They feel God brought him/her there, and he/she should stay until the Lord leads him/her away. And then there are those who always take the side of the underdog. You pit these three groups together against those who feel the staff member needs to go, and you have the potential for real division and conflict . . . and loss of members.

A time of transition can also be a time of regression. If the previous pastor has introduced change to the church, the leaders are apt to revert to their old ways of doing things because it is more comfortable to them. Thus any progress made by the last pastor will become null and void. This is especially true of small churches, or if the pastor has not stayed for an extended time.

I tell young pastors that unless they intend to stay at a church for a long time, not to make too many changes. This is because people don't like change; and second, as soon as they leave the people will go right back to their old ways.

Times of transition can also be times of conflict in the church. Nature abhors a vacuum and so does the church. With the shepherd gone, people, (often good people) rush in to fill the leadership void. In so doing, they often offend other members of the congregation and deep resentments result.

There's a classic example of this in the third epistle of John. In its beginnings, the church had a shortage of trained pastors and was often served by traveling preachers—missionaries. It was the custom and the obligation of the church to offer hospitality to these traveling preachers and provide financial assistance as they continued their ministry.

In this particular church one of its members, Diotrephes, was someone "who loves to be first" (3 John 1:9).

He had asserted leadership in the church and was stifling its missionary spirit. Through gossip, slander, and intimidation he was imposing his will on the church. He was hampering the spread of the gospel and he had created deep resentment and division in the church.

This was not the last church to be hurt by overly ambitious people intoxicated with new positions of leadership and power.

The Bible also gives us an example of a healthy transition in the church. In the wilderness when Moses died, the mantle of leadership falls to Joshua (Deuteronomy 34:5–9; Joshua 1:1–9). The Scriptures say that Moses died without being able to enter into the Promised Land. He is buried in an unmarked grave on a lonely mountainside, overlooking the land he will never enter. The funeral was planned and attended only by God and his angels—no marker on the grave; no flowers; no weeping; just God and the angels.

After a period of mourning, the spotlight shifted to Joshua, the new leader. He had been appointed by God (Numbers 27:18) and anointed by Moses. With new leadership established, the Lord told Joshua, ". . . get ready to cross the Jordan River . . ." The leadership had changed but the mission was the same; to take the Promised Land. Then the Lord gave Joshua this promise, "Have I not commanded you? Be strong and courageous. Do not be terrified; do not be discouraged, for the LORD your God will be with you wherever you go." (Joshua 1:9).

Three truths emerge from this experience which, if grasped, can help any group navigate a time of transition successfully. They are:

> ⟩ Our lives are in God's hands.
> ⟩ The workers die but the work goes on.
> ⟩ The leaders change but the mission remains the same.

▬ Need a Nudge from God? ▬

First, our leader's lives are in God's hands.

The Scriptures state simply, "And Moses the servant of the LORD died there in Moab, as the LORD had said" (Deut. 34:5). Moses didn't die because he was old or because he was sick. He died because God said so.

Alfred Lord Tennyson said of his friend, Percy Shelley, "God's finger touch'd him, and he slept."[1] That's true of all of us. Our lives, day by day, are in the hands of the Lord.

William Henley, in his poem "Invictus" writes:

> It matters not how straight the gate,
> How charges with punishment the scroll.
> I am the master of my fate,
> I am the captain of my soul.[2]

I don't know as much about life and death as I used to, but I know one thing that is not true. I am *not* the master of my fate. I am *not* the captain of my soul. *And neither are you.* We are not in control of many of the events in our lives. *We are in control only of our response to them.*

James, in his epistle, paints a picture of businessmen pouring over a map of the Mediterranean world. They are planning future business ventures and investments, but they do it without considering God. James writes,

> Now listen, you who say, "Today or tomorrow we will go to this or that city, spend a year there, carry on business and make money." Why, you do not even know what will happen tomorrow. What is your life? You are a mist that appears for a little while and then vanishes. Instead, you ought to say, "If it is the Lord's will, we will live and do this or that.
>
> JAMES 4:13–15

This is just another way of saying all our lives are in God's hands. We live only if God wills. Widely understood, this should give us a sense of purpose and significance like nothing else.

On March 30, 1981, President Ronald Reagan was leaving the Washington Hilton Hotel when John Hinckley, Jr. attempted to assassinate him. Three shots rang out and immediately a Secret Service agent shoved President Reagan into a car and fell on him, instructing the driver to go to Washington University Hospital. The president didn't realize he had been shot, thinking the pain he felt was from the fall and the pressure of the Secret Service agent on top of him. But by the time he arrived at the hospital, he had lost one-third of his blood supply. Several major blood vessels had been severed and he had briefly lost his blood pressure and pulse.

Dr. Benjamin Aaron, the chief of cardio-thoracic surgery at George Washington University Hospital, made a quick decision. He told his associates, "In my opinion we stand a good chance of losing him if the bleeding isn't stopped." His decision was that they must operate immediately.

When Dr. Aaron finally retrieved the bullet, it was resting against the wall of his left lung, less than a-half-inch away from his pulsing heart.

FBI ballistics tests revealed that it was a specially designed bullet used for big-game hunting. The bullet was aptly named "the Devastator." It was made to flatten out and cause maximum damage as it ripped through the body. In addition, the tip of the bullet was filled with a chemical called "lead azide" which was designed to explode upon secondary contact with something hard—like a bone. If it exploded it would cause additional damage to a six-inch area in a person's body. Amazingly the bullet did not explode in President Reagan's chest even though the Secret Service agent had landed on him in the limousine and Dr. Aaron had probed for it with his fingers.

Just before he went under the physician's scalpel, the president broke the tension in the room with a loud, clear voice, "I hope you guys are all Republicans!" He smiled when Dr. Giordano, a long-time Democrat replied, "Today, we are all Republicans, Mr. President."

Though he quipped a lot, Reagan saw a divine purpose in all of this. He had been a Christian since he was eleven and was a member of the Disciples of Christ Church. He said he needed a nudge and, "God gave me a wakeup call. Everything I do from this time on, I owe to God. From this time on my time belongs to God." His son Michael said his father told him that, "It was only divine intervention that kept him alive."[3]

God has a divine purpose not only for us as individuals, but also for his church. We all need a nudge from time to time to be reminded that our lives are in his hands. Hopefully it will not take a bullet to remind us of that.

▬ Appointed and Anointed ▬

Second, the workers die but the work goes on.

Moses, Israel's first leader; died and was buried in an unmarked grave on a lonely mountainside. Again, the service was attended only by God and the angels with no marker, or flowers, or anything.

But, Joshua had already been appointed by God and anointed by Moses as the new leader. The Scriptures say, "Now Joshua son of Nun was filled with the spirit of wisdom because Moses had laid his hands on him. So the Israelites listened to him and did what the LORD had commanded Moses" (Deut. 34:9).

That's the way God works. He never leaves his people without leadership. When Billy Graham turned ninety-three a friend said to me, "We need to pick someone to take his place."

I replied, "Only God can raise up somebody to take Graham's place."

I say that with confidence, because God always has. British-born **George Whitfield** (1714–1770) was America's first great evangelist. His father died when he was a child so he was reared by a single mother. She was an innkeeper and he spent his early days helping her with the guests. He entered Oxford and quickly became friends with fellow student John Wesley who founded the Methodist church. At the age of twenty he experienced the new birth and became a minister. Wesley was a gifted organizer but Whitfield soon became the most popular preacher in England.

He became an ordained minister of the Church of England. But soon, because of his enthusiasm and his emphasis on personal conversion, he (along with Wesley) was excluded from preaching in the Anglican Church. He began to preach in an open field a few miles outside Bristol and soon was attracting crowds of five-to-six thousand coal miners at 5:00 a.m. before they went to work. These were people who had never been inside a traditional church.

Whitfield once preached to an estimated crowd of 80,000 in Hyde Park, and he did it without the benefit of amplification. After great success in England, he crossed the Atlantic thirteen times (six-and-a-half round trips) and preached up and down the Atlantic seaboard. His dramatic sermons, often lasting two hours, consistently drew crowds of five, ten, and occasionally twenty-thousand people who came from miles around to hear him preach.

Whitfield's bold, direct, and enthusiastic preaching lit revival fires all across New England. When he died at the age of fifty-six on September 29, 1770 at Newberry Court, Massachusetts; the flame of evangelism flickered but it did not go out. In less than twenty-two years, America's second greatest evangelist would be born.

Charles G. Finney (1792–1872) is considered by some to be America's greatest evangelist. He drew crowds upwards of 10,000 people. Whole cities were converted when he preached.

Finney grew up in a non-Christian home. He had never heard a prayer till he prayed one himself. He had never read the Bible till he bought one at the age of twenty-nine. He was a lawyer by profession. He also had a good singing voice, so the Presbyterian minister asked him to lead the choir, even though he was not a believer. He bought a Bible to check the references the pastor gave in his sermons.

Finney began to secretly read the Bible, and while walking in the woods one day, God spoke to him and asked, "What are you waiting on? Are you endeavoring to work out righteousness on your own?" He said, "I saw Christ's finished work and a voice said, 'Will you accept me now?'" He said, "I will" and surrendered to Christ.[4]

He knew if he accepted Christ he would preach the gospel. He gave up his law practice immediately. A client whom he was to represent in a trial that morning came in and he said, "Deacon Barney, I have a retainer from the Lord Jesus Christ to plead his cause and I cannot plead yours."[5] (And he dropped the client then and there.)

Finney once preached seventy successive evenings to crowds that averaged 1,500–2,500. On another occasion he took a fifteen-month pastorate in New York to show that evangelism was possible at the highest level, even in a pastorate.

When he died at the age of eighty, some believed that the fires of evangelism had been extinguished in America. But remember, *the workers die but the work goes on.* Before Finney died, the Lord had raised up the next great evangelist, D.L. Moody.

D.L. Moody (1837–99) would also preach to crowds of 10,000 or more. He once rented a circus tent at the World's Fair in Chicago and drew greater crowds at night than the circus did during the day. He grew up on a farm in Northfield, Massachusetts, quit school at sixteen and moved to Boston to work as a salesman in his uncle's shoe store.

One of his uncle's rules was that he had to attend church, and so Moody reluctantly attended the local Congregational Church. His Sunday School teacher, Edward Kimble, called on him at work, caught him in the stockroom and witnessed to him. He accepted Christ at the age of eighteen.

Moody's ambition was to make $100,000 so he moved to Chicago. There he accepted a Sunday School class in a mission church and began to reach poor children with the gospel. The crowds grew and he was soon speaking to a packed house. He gave up his worldly ambitions and gave himself to preaching the gospel. In time he became a powerful and popular evangelist in both America and England.

In Brooklyn, he rented a skating rink and preached to 6,000 people a day. In Pennsylvania, he rented a freight depot and preached to 10,000 people every night. He conducted 8:00 a.m. services five-days-a-week and people lined up at 4:30 a.m. to gain admission. Though he weighed 280 pounds, used poor grammar, and had an unkempt appearance; he still reached thousands for Christ.

Surely no one could carry the mantel of evangelism after Moody. But, remember, *the workers die but the work goes on*. The Lord had already groomed Billy Sunday as the next great evangelist in America.

Billy Sunday (1862–1935) would sweep the country like a Kansas tornado. Sunday's father died in the Civil War, four months before he was born. His family was poor and his mother kept the boys until she could no longer afford them. When Billy was six-years-of-age she placed them in an orphanage. He stayed there until he was fourteen. He had some religious training but he never responded to the gospel.

At the age of fourteen he went out on his own. He was a good athlete and eventually played professional baseball with the Chicago White Sox. At the age of twenty-five he was with a group of players on the streets of Chicago when a friend invited them to attend the Pacific Garden Rescue Mission. That night he trusted Christ as his savior.

He eventually joined J. Wilbur Chapman, who was an evangelist. He learned the trade by putting up tents, unfolding chairs, and making an occasional talk. When Chapman went back into the pastorate, people began to ask Billy Sunday to preach. The doors were opened and his evangelistic ministry was launched.

His tabernacle meetings drew crowds of 25,000 people and he could be heard in those meetings without the benefit of a public address system. By the time he died at the age of seventy-three, the Lord had already laid his hands on a young Billy Graham.

Billy Graham, born in 1918, has preached to more people than any other man in history. He grew up on a dairy farm in North Carolina, the son of devout Presbyterian parents. He was a typical high school student who had no interest in religion and aspired to be a professional baseball player. At the age of sixteen he attended a revival meeting where Mordecai Ham was preaching. He sat in the choir so he could see the girls and wouldn't have to look the preacher in the face. But God had other plans, and that night Billy was converted to Christ.

At the age of thirty he began to work with the Youth for Christ movement. In 1949 the movement rented a tent and sponsored a three-week crusade in Los Angeles, California. Several prominent people came to Christ. Randolph Hearst ordered his news people to cover the story. Graham was launched into a nationwide, and then a worldwide ministry.

How else could it have happened except through the providence of God? *The workers keep dying but the work goes on and on.* Look at these men. They were from every walk of life: college students, lawyers, shoe salesmen, professional athletes, and high school students. They were from various denominations: Methodists, Presbyterians, Congregationalists, and Baptists. The important thing was not their background, nor their denomination, but rather their commitment to Christ.

Bishop E.W. Johnson, in a radio sermon said this concerning ministers, "Some were called, some were sent, and some just went." These were all men who heard and answered the call and God used them mightily. They were sent by God.

God always has another leader ready. They have already been appointed and anointed.

The loss of a leader never catches God by surprise. He is always way ahead of us.

━ Enlarge Your Vision ━

Third, leadership changes but the mission remains the same.

Twenty-one times in the Old Testament the Lord told Moses that he would take the Israelites to the land of milk and honey. Though Moses was not permitted to enter in, the mission remained the same: take the Promised Land.

During a time of transition it is easy to lose our focus as God's people, and to turn inward instead of outward to a lost world. Our mission is clear. It has not changed since Jesus met with his disciples following his resurrection. He gave them the great commission saying: "Therefore go and make disciples of all nations, baptizing them in the name of the Father and of the Son and of the Holy Spirit, and teaching them to obey everything I have commanded you. And surely I am with you always, to the very end of the age" (Matthew 28:19–20).

Our mission is ever and always the same. Bring them in, build them up, and send them out. And we are to stay everlastingly at that until Jesus comes again.

We must never lose sight of our mission. George Shultz, who served as Secretary of State under President Ronald Reagan, would routinely bring U.S. Ambassadors into his office where he kept a large globe. "Show me the country you will be representing," he would say. Most of the time, the diplomat would give the globe a spin, abruptly halting it in motion to indicate Botswana, Bhutan, Brunei or whatever country he'd be calling home for the next few years. Shultz would say, "Never forget, you're over there in that country, but your country is the United States. You're there to represent us."[6]

Remember who you work for. We are ambassadors for Christ. We must never lose sight of our first loyalty.

In pre-World War II Germany, as Hitler increased his military strength, England was warned again and again by its ambassador of what was happening. At Hitler's insistence those critical of him were recalled, and eventually Sir Nevil Henderson was given the assignment as Great Britain's ambassador to Germany. He became fast friends with Herman Goring and forgot his duty and his country's standards. Thus he failed in his essential responsibility to represent his country.[7]

That can happen to churches also. They become too friendly with the world and cease to represent Christ's kingdom.

I have a friend who worked for a cable television company. His travels often took him through East Texas to Louisiana. On his journey to DeRidder, Louisiana he often stopped in Newton, Texas to get a bologna sandwich. Newton is a small East Texas town of 2,500 people.

It was during the Cuban Missile Crisis of 1962 when he stopped one day and heard a group of old men on the courthouse square. One of them said, "You know, if those things hit, this will be one of the first places hit." One of his friends asked, "What makes you think that?" He replied, "Well, this is the county seat."

That man lived in a small world. It consisted primarily of Newton County, Texas. We must never forget that we are ambassadors for Christ and our mission is to carry the gospel to the whole world. For the believer, the center of the universe has shifted, the circumference has expanded. It is no longer "us and ours," but "them and theirs." It is the whole world.

And as we go, we can remember the promise of God to Joshua, ". . . Be strong and courageous. Do not be terrified; do not be discouraged, for the LORD your God will be with you wherever you go" (Josh.1:9).

Or if you prefer the words of Jesus, ". . . And surely I am with you always, to the very end of the age" (Matt. 28:20).

Our loyalty is to the Lord and not to any one leader.

Our vision is for the world and not just for our community.

Keep that in mind and the transition will be better.

NOTES

1. http://theotherpages.org/poems/books/tennyson/tennyson06.html. Accessed 5/23/2014.

2. William Ernest Henley, *Echoes of Life and Death* (Portland, Maine: Thomas B. Mosher, 1908), 7.

3. Mary Beth Brown, *The Faith of Ronald Reagan* (Nashville: Thomas Nelson, 2004), 2–16.

4. Charles G. Finney, *Memoirs of Rev. Charles G. Finney* (New York: A.S. Barnes & Company, 1876), 14.

5. Charles E. Hambrick-Stowe, *Charles G. Finney and the Spirit of American Evangelicalism* (Grand Rapids, Michigan: Wm. B. Eerdmans Publishing Co., 1996), 19.

6. http://www.booknotes.org/FullPage.aspx?SID=44051–1. Accessed 5/27/2014.

7. William Manchester, *The Last Lion: Winston Spencer Churchill: Alone, 1932–1940* (Boston, MA: Little, Brown, and Company, 1988), 88.

12

The Call of God

But you, keep your head in all situations, endure hardship, do the work of an evangelist, discharge all the duties of your ministry.

2 Timothy 4:5

It was said of the clergy in England in the 1600s, "Many members of the clergy were absent from their churches, often more concerned with hunting and card playing. This led to the neglect of the spiritual needs of the congregation."[1]

Substitute golf and the computer for hunting and card playing; and maybe things haven't changed all that much since then.

A faithful church leader wrote of his pastor, "He doesn't do any work . . . period. He studies, does sermons he probably got from one of his buddies and modifies them . . . He plays golf three to four days a week . . . is never at the church . . . Doesn't do visits to the hospital unless it's some really close friends or a donor . . . and his personality is about as warm as an ice cube. It's hard on old-timers like me who had a *pastor*."

The chairman of a pastor search committee wrote of their finding, "the only one that the majority feel might be acceptable is in his mid-fifties, wants a week off every quarter, two days off during the week, and wants that respected. That won't work."

I wish I had a dollar for every letter or call I have had like these. If their assessment is correct, it is no wonder our churches are in decline.

To be a pastor is a singular honor but it is also an awesome responsibility. It is as Thomas Jefferson described the presidency, "A splendid misery."[2]

Realistically we need a new assessment of the call of God to be a minister. Simply put it is to:

) Preach the word.
) Love the people.
) Lead the church.

▬ Fed Up With Not Being Fed ▬

The first call of a pastor is to preach the word.

Jesus was first and foremost a preacher. He sent his first disciples out to preach. And the Apostle Paul's admonition to his younger protégé was "Preach the Word" (2 Timothy 4:2). The word of course is the word of God, the Scriptures.

It is safe to say that the church rises and falls with preaching. When preaching is strong, the church advances. When it is weak and anemic, the church falters. So, the pastor has no more important and challenging task than preaching. It is through preaching that people are saved. It is through preaching that the flock is fed.

Sheep like to be fed. They almost never resist. But they are soon fed up with not being fed and look elsewhere for greener pastures.

Effective preaching doesn't have to be spectacular. It seldom is. But it does have to be Bible-centered. The preacher's singular task is to tell people what God says in a simple, straightforward, sincere way. Everything else is illustration and application.

Preaching is both a gift and a discipline. It takes hard work to dig a sermon out and hard work to deliver it. But the most essential thing about good preaching is that it be authentic.

I once visited with Russell Scott, seeking financial support for Texas Cowboy Churches. I had never met Mr. Scott but his insurance agent took me to meet him.

After we visited a while, I told him the purpose of my visit was to ask him for financial support for the Cowboy Church movement. He responded, "Tell me about the Cowboy Churches. I have seen their signs on the highway but don't know anything about them."

I explained that they appeal primarily to people in the western-heritage culture; that most of their structures are metal buildings, not elaborate cathedrals; that they most often begin with a couple hundred people; and that they average baptizing thirty-five people each year (eighty percent of those baptized being adults).

Immediately "Scotty" was interested. He said, "I like that. I am interested in reaching people for Christ." Then he told me his story.

He had been reared in a Lutheran home and was christened as a baby. But he had never had a personal experience with Jesus Christ. In college he had some friends who kept talking about a revival meeting in their church and he decided to attend one of the services with them. The preacher was an old man who had been called to preach while he was plowing. He had no formal education and taught himself to read and write.

When he started reading his text that night he read so haltingly, that Scotty said, "I wondered what I had gotten myself into." When he finished he reached up and took off his eyeglasses, closed his Bible, and said, "When I came here today I forgot my glasses and I had to borrow these. And I forgot my Bible and I had to borrow this Bible. But what I've got to say to you ain't borrowed."

Scotty said that he was moved by the old preacher's sincerity, and that he put his faith in Christ that night and was saved.

Authentic preaching ain't borrowed preaching. It grows out of the preacher's own experience, his own walk with God, and his own study of God's word. In short "he owns it." He doesn't borrow it from some computer service. The authentic preacher studies all week and preaches thirty minutes, not vice versa.

Winston Churchill, the late Prime Minister of Great Britain who almost single-handedly inspired British resistance to Hitler during World War II with his rousing speeches, said, "The key to a speaker's impact on his audience is sincerity. Before he can inspire them with any emotion he must be swayed by it himself . . . Before he can move them to tears his own must flow. To convince them he must himself believe."[3]

As to simplicity and style, Churchill said, "If you have an important point to make, don't try to be subtle or clever, use a pile driver. Hit the point once. Then come back and hit it again. Then hit it a third time—a tremendous whack."[4]

Simplicity, sincerity, and straightforwardness are the keys to authenticity. It is harder to move people by preaching today than ever before because the average American experiences 3,000 marketing messages a day. While it's harder, it's still possible. Authenticity is the key.

The Shepherd Should Smell Like the Sheep

The second calling of a pastor is to love the people.

It's a well-worn statement, "People don't care how much you know until they know how much you care." But it's just as true today as it was the first day it was first spoken. If people ever get the idea that you put your interests above theirs, your effectiveness is over. For that reason, the pastor must be among the people, available to the people, ministering to them, and serving them.

After a while, the shepherd ought to smell like the sheep. The biggest cause of failure in the ministry is not immorality or poor preaching. The biggest culprit is the failure to care for people and the inability to get along with people.

Pastors could learn a lesson—a valuable lesson—about people skills from Herb Kelleher, co-founder and chairman emeritus and former CEO of Southwest Airlines. He and another businessman founded the company in 1971 and operated it as one of the most successful and profitable airlines in the world. Southwest Airlines has more capital than its six biggest competitors combined. Part of the secret is Kelleher himself.

I boarded a plane to Lubbock a couple of years ago and Herb Kelleher was a passenger. Though retired, he stood at the door and welcomed everyone who boarded the plane. Then when the flight landed he stood at the door and shook hands with and thanked everyone for flying Southwest Airlines.

Herb Kelleher didn't have to do that. He could have boarded the plane early, taken a back seat and buried his face in a magazine. No one would have noticed and no one would have faulted him. After all, he was eighty-years-old at the time and retired. But that's not how he built a great airline.

Chuck Swindoll provides another example of how to relate to people. He is the pastor of the Stonebriar Community Church in Frisco, Texas. We all know him as an accomplished writer and radio preacher. His program is carried on 2,100 stations and in fifteen languages. I'm not sure what the attendance is at Stonebriar, but the second week after it began in 1998, the church had 1,200 adults in attendance.

My wife and I attended a service at Stonebriar a couple of years ago and sat at the back section of the sanctuary. We were talking to one another when I heard loud laughter coming from the front of the church. I looked to the front and there was Chuck Swindoll moving through the congregation, shaking hands and laughing with the people.

He didn't have to do that. He could have slipped in with the choir, taken his seat at the rostrum, and no one would have thought anything about it. But that's not who he is and that's not how he built a great church. He loves his people and he spends time among them. That's not always easy to do. Some people are not easy to like. But loving and liking are not the same thing. The late Calvin Miller, in his autobiography wrote (with tongue firmly planted in cheek), "Will Rogers said, 'I never met a man I didn't like' but I suspect he didn't get out all that much. And I'm pretty sure he never pastored a church."[5]

It is often the little things that are most important in building good relationships with people. Jack Nicklaus is perhaps the greatest golfer who has ever lived. At least he has won more major tournaments than anyone, including Tiger Woods. A newspaper reporter asked him about the changes that have taken place in golf over the years. He listed things like equipment, sports psychologists, agents, and larger paychecks.

The thing that troubles him most is the manners or the lack of communication exhibited by the newer generation. Then someone asked him in particular about Tiger Woods. They wanted to know if Tiger called Jack personally when he dropped out of Jack's Memorial Tournament due to a leg injury.

Jack responded that he heard only from Tiger's agent. Then he said, "So every tournament I ever played in, I always dropped the sponsor a note."[6] Nicklaus didn't have to do that. He was the world's greatest golfer and lesser men didn't do such things. But one of the marks of a big man is that he does the little things.

George W. Truett, famed pastor of the First Baptist Church of Dallas for forty-seven years, was granted a six-month leave of absence to serve as a chaplain in Europe during World War I. He worked tirelessly, frequently as much eighteen-hours-a-day. But after preaching as much as six times a day and talking privately with scores of people; he wrote letters far into the night by flickering light. He wrote a personal note to some loved one of every soldier he met from Texas—mother, father, wife, sister, sweetheart, anyone the boy named—and he met soldiers from Texas by the hundreds.

Back in the states word spread (it always does) and Truett became one of the most respected and beloved men in Texas. Any preacher can write himself into the hearts of his people the same way. It just takes time and thought.[7]

My military hero is General George Patton. He said on one occasion, "Wars may be fought with weapons but they are won by men."[8] We've got plenty of machines (weapons) in the modern church—computers, iPads, cell phones, fax machines, projectors, television cameras, and big screens. But they are no substitute for pastors who are among the people doing the work of the ministry.

Make machines your servants, not your master. Don't let them dominate your life. They can't substitute for a personal touch, for being available and involved with people. As I said to one young preacher who wasted hours on the computer every day, "Get off that computer and go to work."

He didn't, and the church eventually fired him.

▬ Rock 'n Roll and Rocking Chair ▬

The third call of a pastor is to lead the church.

Every group I know needs a leader. A team needs a coach. An army needs a commander. A business needs a CEO. And a flock needs a shepherd. Without a leader a church will sit and do nothing and do it very well until Jesus comes. The church must be led to fulfill her mission, to minister to the needy, to reach her potential. That leadership role falls of necessity to the pastor.

Leadership is best learned by example. Ramiro Romo, the grandfather of Tony Romo, the quarterback of the Dallas Cowboys, is a deacon in the Catholic church in Crockett, Texas. He relates, "I was a shepherd in the mountains of Mexico as a boy. And I noticed that when one of the shepherds walked in front of his goats, they followed him. And when he lay down to take a nap, the goats went to sleep too. People are the same way—if you treat them well, they won't go away from you."

Out in front; wide awake; sensitive to people; this is the secret to leadership.

I have been the interim pastor of the First Baptist Church of Tyler twice. The first time (1996–97) the church had a high attendance of 1,365 and a healthy average of approximately 1,000. By the time I became their interim pastor for the second time (2009–2011), the church was averaging 750 or less. It had been in a slow decline for over ten years. They had averaged only seventy-five additions to the church per year for the past five years, and the church was averaging forty deaths per year. In addition, a number of people were transferring to other churches.

This grand old church had been established in 1848. They were anchored to their downtown location but they bought property south of town and established another campus. It was one church in two locations. The South Campus was averaging 300 in attendance and Downtown was averaging 450. The worship style at the South Campus was contemporary and Downtown was traditional.

I jokingly said, "Out South we have a rock 'n roll church and Downtown we have a rocking chair church." I think you get the picture. The South Campus was filled with race-horses and the Downtown Campus was filled with plow horses. Both are perfectly good animals, but they move at a different gait. A racehorse is good for about five minutes, but a plow horse can be hooked up to a plow early in the morning and when the sun sets it's still pulling its load.

The first staff meeting of my interim I told the staff that I wanted the name, address, and phone number of every visitor on my computer by 2:00 p.m. Sunday after-noon. I intended to call all the visitors and welcome them to our church. From the information I gathered from those calls I would make visitation assignments to each of the staff members.

To my amazement, the next Sunday the staff sent me the names of forty visitors from the South Campus and fifty from the Downtown Campus, a total of ninety in all. Admittedly some of them had been visiting for months but had not been contacted. That prompted me to write in the pastor's column of the church newsletter, "This is not a *declining* church. It is a *reclining* church. You people have gone to sleep at the switch. You need to wake up and smell the coffee."

At the next staff meeting I said to the staff, "You obviously have a product people want, but you haven't been closing the sale." Then I assigned two prospects to every staff member and expected them to report back at the next staff meeting.

As a result, 200 people joined our church over the next year. When we went out, they came in. When people started joining the church I said to the staff, "These people have been out there all along but you haven't been out there."

Leadership is nothing more than seeing what needs to be done; figuring out how to do it; and getting people to join you in the effort.

Another illustration from the same church will help. Shortly after beginning with them I realized they were running a budget deficit of $10,000 a week. By that time they were $300,000 behind in their annual receipts. The finance committee had established a $500,000 line of credit at the beginning of the year and the church was on schedule to use it all by year's end.

I proposed we set a Harvest Day attendance and offering campaign for the Sunday before Thanksgiving. The attendance campaign would be built around the theme "No Empty Chairs" and every class would be challenged to fill every chair that day. The overall goal was to have 1,000 people in Sunday School.

We then proposed a one-day-offering to get the church out of debt and on solid financial footing. I promised if they would get us out of debt I would keep us out.

The offering plan was simple. I encouraged every child to give $5.00 from money they earned by their own work. It was not to come from their allowance. I encouraged every teenager to give $25.00 that they earned on their own. I pointed out that was less than the cost of a hamburger and a coke each week for a month.

Then I challenged every couple to give $100 a year for each year they had been married. Cathy and I had been married fifty-five years so I wrote a check for $5,500 and postdated it a month ahead to Harvest Day.

We had fun in the promotion. One Sunday I asked how many people had been married fifty years or more. Hands went up everywhere. Then I said, "We have the TV cameras on so we've got you on film."

Then one Sunday I pointed out that $100 a year was only $1.94 a week or 27 cents a day. I asked, "Men, where else can you get your meals cooked, your house cleaned, your clothes washed, and your children cared for at 27 cents a day? So lean over to that little woman and say, 'Honey you are worth every penny of it', then pay up."

I knew we had some widows who were living on Social Security and single moms who were living on a shoestring. They couldn't give that amount. I didn't want anyone to feel guilty if they were unable to contribute at the stated level.

I reminded them of 2 Corinthians 8:12, "For if the willingness is there, the gift is acceptable according to what one has, not according to what he does not have." Then I said, "If you would if you could, if you want to but can't, that counts just as much with the Lord as if you give it."

Harvest Day came and we had torrential rains. I was sure the whole effort would be a wash out. But to my surprise, we had 956 in Sunday School and cash gifts of $720,000.

I told the staff the next day I wanted this to be a teaching moment. It showed what can be done when you have 3 things:

› A clear goal.
› A workable plan.
› Enthusiastic promotion.

That's Leadership 101.

Leadership begins with a clear vision, i.e., seeing what needs to be done, knowing where you want to go, or what you want to accomplish. As Carl Sandberg said, "Nothing happens unless first a dream."[9] The clearer and more precise the vision, the better.

In rallying England to arms in the opening days of World War II, Prime Minister Winston Churchill said to the House of Commons in June 1941, "I have only one purpose, the destruction of Hitler, and my life is much simplified thereby."[10] England responded to his clear call and Hitler was eventually defeated.

Then there must be a plan. T. Boone Pickens, a highly successful Texas oil man, gave the federal government fifty-eight million dollars to develop a national energy plan so we could be independent of foreign oil. He explained, "My dad once said to me, 'Son, a fool with a plan can beat a genius with no plan.'"[11]

Finally, people must be motivated to action. If you have a clear and worthwhile goal, if you are respected by your people, and your promotion is enthusiastic and optimistic; people will respond to you. In World War II Prime Minister Winston Churchill of England inspired the nation with his own stern and resolute fortitude. That's what leaders do.

There are several practical keys to wise leadership worth noting:

A wise leader not only knows what to do, but also knows what not to do.

The Ark of the Covenant in the Old Testament was sacred. It was not to be touched. Once when it was being moved, one of the oxen pulling the cart stumbled causing the cart and ark to tilt. Uzzah, one of the cart drivers reached up to steady the ark and he died. (2 Samuel 6:6–7)

In every church or organization there are some things considered sacred and untouchable. A good leader is first a historian. He learns what is "untouchable" and leaves it alone. He doesn't risk his leadership on something foolish. A wise leader also seeks the counsel of wise people before he acts. Rehoboam was the heir apparent to King Solomon. Solomon had abused his power in the latter years of his reign and the people chafed under his leadership. Before they ratified the new king, the elders of Israel asked Rehoboam how he intended to rule. The older wiser men said to him, "If today you will be a servant to these people and serve them and give them a favorable answer, they will always be your servants" (1 Kings 12:7; also 2 Chronicles 10:7).

That is good advice for any leader. Serve the people, seek their well-being, and speak to them kindly.

Then Rehoboam asked the advice of younger, inexperienced men and they said, "Don't knuckle under, Boss. Tell them you'll be far harder on them than your father ever thought" (1 Kings 12:10–11).

He ignored the older, wiser men; took the advice of the younger men, and the elders rejected him as king. It split the kingdom. More than one pastor has lost his leadership and split a church for the same reason.

A wise leader does not set himself above the people. Matt Doherty, former head basketball coach at Southern Methodist University, also served as head coach at the University of North Carolina; one of the top basketball schools in America.

But he was fired from that job. The reason? He says he should have kept his assistants in place and should have let coaches Dean Smith and Bill Guthridge, his predecessors, serve as a board of directors for him. "I was too independent." An independent spirit can be deadly for any leader.

And finally, a wise leader enlists the support of the right people before he ventures too far.

Drayton McLane of McLane Foods said that Sam Walton, founder of Wal-Mart, called on him wanting to buy his company. Mr. Walton wanted to begin selling groceries in Wal-Mart and needed a food company to do so.

Drayton told him his company was not for sale, and furthermore he told Sam that people would never buy groceries from a large warehouse-type store. Sam said, "Drayton, I didn't ask for your opinion. I came to share my big idea with you." Drayton said his business was still not for sale.

That night when Drayton got home, his wife asked, "What's this big idea Sam Walton came to see you about?" He asked how she knew about the big idea. Then she told him on the flight back to Arkansas that Mr. Walton had called her to explain his offer and to encourage her to encourage Drayton to take it.

To make a long story short, Drayton sold to Wal-Mart.

A wise leader always enlists the support of the power brokers before he ventures out, if it is possible.

A Latin proverb says, "Words move people, examples lead them." The preacher's voice, backed up by a good life, is his greatest asset. His voice—like the voice of a politician, a general, or a coach—is his primary way of leading. But he must also set an example. Both are essential.

President Teddy Roosevelt once said of former President John Tyler, "He has been called a mediocre man, but that is unwarranted flattery. He was a man of monumental littleness."[12]

This is not a day for ministerial mediocrity. We need to "man up." The times demand it and the stakes are eternal.

Pastor, if God has called you, ". . . discharge all the duties of your ministry" (2 Timothy 4:5).

Preach the word.

Love the people.

Lead the church.

N O T E S

1. Kevin Belmonte, *A Journey Through the Life of William Wilberforce* (Green Forest, AR: New Leaf Press, 2006), 68.

2. Jon Meacham, *Thomas Jefferson: The Art of Power* (New York, NY: Random House, 2012), 305.

3. William Manchester, *The Last Lion: Winston Spencer Churchill: Alone, 1932–1940* (Boston, MA: Little, Brown, and Company, 1988), 208.

4. Richard Langworth, *Churchill By Himself: The Definitive Collection* (New York, NY: Public Affairs, 2008), 73.

5. Calvin Miller, *Letters to a Young Pastor* (Colorado Springs, CO: David C. Cook, 2011), 78.

6. http://www.thebraziltimes.com/story/1432075.html. Accessed 5/27/2014.

7. Powhatan W. James, *George W. Truett* (Nashville: Broadman Press, 1945), 141.

8. http://www.generalpatton.com/quotes/index3.html. Accessed 5/27/2014.

9. Carl Sandburg, "Washington Monument by Night" in *The Complete Poems of Carl Sandburg*, Revised edition (Orlando, Florida: Harcourt, Brace and Co., 1970), 282.

10. Winston Churchill (Speech, Chequers, England, June 21, 1941).

11. http://www.nytimes.com/2008/08/03/magazine/03wwlnQ4-t.html?fta=y&_r=0. Accessed 5/27/2014.

12. Theodore Roosevelt, *The Words of Theodore Roosevelt: Thomas Hart Benson* (New York: NY: Charles Scribner's Sons, 1906), 227.

Conclusion

After sixty years of ministry I have adopted a new life verse, 1 Timothy 1:12 (KJV), "And I thank Christ Jesus our Lord, who hath enabled me, for that he counted me faithful, putting me into the ministry . . ."

After these many years in ministry, there are two things of which I am certain.

First, the Lord put me in the ministry.

It was on an ordinary Sunday, in an ordinary church, listening to an ordinary preacher preach an ordinary sermon, that God did an extraordinary thing in my life. And that's the way he ordinarily does it.

I remember it as though it was yesterday; I was sitting in the First Baptist Church of Port Arthur, Texas minding my own business. I was alone because nobody in my family went to church—not at Christmas, not at Easter, not for a wedding, not for a funeral, not ever; when figuratively speaking—Jesus walked down the aisle, tapped me on the shoulder, and said, "Come and follow me and I will make you a fisher of men."

That's the only touch and the only voice that could have moved me to become a minister. I have doubted many things through the years but I have never doubted that God called me into the ministry.

Second, I know Jesus has enabled me to do the things I have done.

I am not super smart or multi-talented and I could not have been involved in all the things I have been involved in without his help. I was born in the backwoods of East Texas; I grew up in the back alleys of Port Arthur; and I was usually at the back of my class. At the end of class one day in my senior year, my English teacher stopped me as we left the classroom and said to me, "Paul, I know you want to be a preacher and go to college, I want to tell you, you won't ever make it." But Mrs. Goldman didn't take into account what God can do when we commit our lives to him.

What I don't understand is why he trusted me with the riches of the gospel. It was an act of his grace pure and simple. There is no other explanation.

Now days, the dominate mode of my life is gratitude, not only gratitude to God but also to my Baptist family. There is an old African saying, "If you want to travel fast, travel alone. If you want to travel far, travel with a group." When I was a young man I was in a hurry. I wasn't sure where I was going, but I was in a hurry to get there and I didn't need anybody's help. I would have made a great independent preacher, but I wouldn't have gotten very far. When I joined the Baptist family it gave me a sense of belonging, inspiration, and encouragement, and a world vision.

If I had just one word to give to young ministers it would be this: stay faithful to your calling and stay with the Baptist family.

Another verse that has meant a great deal to me in recent days is Exodus 23:20–21, where the Lord said to Moses: "See, I am sending an angel ahead of you to guard you along the way and to bring you to the place I have prepared. Pay attention to him and listen to what he says."

I don't know much about angels. I never saw one or talked to one. But I do know that God sent someone ahead to guard me on my way and to bring me to the places he wanted me to go. I am still trying to pay attention to him and listen to what he has to say.

The Lord has been faithful to me in my long walk and I want to be faithful to him to the end.